Dear Roy

May your
filled with wonderful
new beginnings!
    Warmly,
    Glenna Salsbury

The Art of the Fresh Start

Health Communications, Inc.
Deerfield Beach, Florida

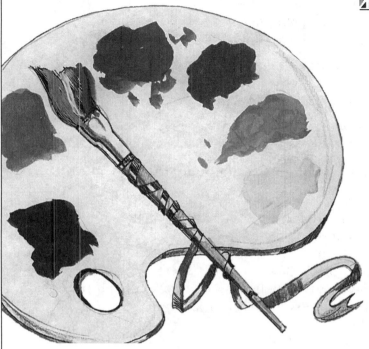

THE ART OF THE FRESH START

How to Make and Keep Your
New Year's Resolutions for a Lifetime

Glenna Salsbury

We would like to acknowledge the following publishers for permission to reprint the following material:

Adapted from *Those Not-So-Still Small Voices*, © 1993 by Thom Hunter. Used by permission of NavPress, Colorado Springs, Co. All rights reserved. For copies call 1-800-366-7788.

Leadership Jazz and *Leadership Is an Art*, by Max DePree. Reprinted by permission of *DOUBLEDAY*, a division of Bantam Doubleday Dell Publishing Group, Inc.

The Fifth Discipline, by Peter Senge. Reprinted by permission of *DOUBLEDAY*, a division of Doubleday Dell Publishing Group, Inc.

Library of Congress Cataloging-in-Publication Data

Salsbury, Glenna, (date)
  The art of the fresh start : how to make and keep your New Year's resolutions for a lifetime / Glenna Salsbury.
    p.   cm.
  ISBN 1-55874-364-2 (trade paper)
  1. Self-actualization (Psychology)   2. Self-perception.
  3. Change (Psychology)   4. Salsbury, Glenna, 1937-
  I. Title.
  BF637.S4S24   1995
  158' . 1--dc20   95-40424
                                                          CIP

©1995 Glenna Salsbury
ISBN 1-55874-364-2

Publisher: Health Communications, Inc.
          3201 S.W. 15th Street
          Deerfield Beach, Florida 33442-8190

Cover design by Jose Villavicencio
Cover illustration by Sylvia D. Kowalczyk

To my dad, whose legacy of love and faith continues to impact my life and the lives of others.

Contents

Preface

I remember the precise moment I received the inspiration for this book. I felt a gentle nudge in my solar plexus as I gazed out of my window seat on the TWA flight from New York City to Phoenix, and I knew *He* was speaking to me. Nevertheless, this book is not ethereal. Rather, it answers a concrete question that plagues us all.

In January of 1995 I appeared on *Good Morning America* with the host, Charles Gibson, and two of my colleagues, Zig Ziglar and Les Brown. As professional speakers who focus on motivation, we were answering the question, "How is it possible to keep one's New Year's resolutions?" And, naturally, "Why are so many people unable to keep their resolutions?"

To prepare for the interview I had given much thought to the questions. One truth seemed overwhelmingly clear to me, based on my own life experience:

These resolutions almost always are artificial in that they are based on what we think we ought to do. The solution is to create commitments that are congruent with the real you, the inner you.

This truth opens a yawning cavern for most of us. The lack of inner awareness is part of the reason for increased stress, anxiety, divorce, unhappiness, suicide, drugs and every other kind of social problem.

So the bigger question, as opposed to simply learning to keep your New Year's resolutions, is:

How is it possible to really know yourself and then learn to consistently live a life that is congruent and true to your unique self?

During the *Good Morning America* interview I answered questions about the cause of failure. In the brief moments on the show I hinted at the solution:

God has designed you uniquely and planted specific desires in your heart. As you discover His purpose for your life you will walk naturally into the resolutions and commitments that support your desires.

But, there is so much to know about the "how" of this process. As I pondered the how at 35,000 feet in the air, I realized that these were the very truths and practical principles that the Creator has worked into my life. In fact, my passion as a speaker is to communicate the life-changing eternal insights that lift people above their circumstances. On January 2, 1995, I resolved to write these principles in book form for you.

As I considered what to do about finding a publisher, I slipped into the mental gyrations and fear syndrome that you will read about in these pages. My mind began to explain that it will take years to find a publisher and get the book in print. Then I remembered afresh that the desire was springing from my heart, thus the doors would open because the Heavenly Designer was at work in this. That transfer into the spirit, out of the chaotic mind, is precisely the principle on which the book is based.

The very next thought that came to me out of my transformed mind, a principle also in this book, was:

Your story has been an inherent part of the success of the New York Times *bestseller* Chicken Soup for the Soul. *Why not call that publisher and share your sense of direction?*

And, thanks to the wisdom and leadership of Christine Belleris, acquisitions editor, Health Communications, Inc. called me back with an enthusiastic commitment to publish *The Art of the Fresh Start.*

Finally, isn't it interesting that at the close of the *Good Morning America* interview Charles Gibson turned to me and said, "So what is your New Year's resolution, Glenna?" "I'd like to finish writing my book," I responded. That's the power residing in the principles you'll find in this book!

Glenna Salsbury

Acknowledgments

Love fires my life and I have been surrounded by an abundant supply of this precious commodity.

My three daughters. Monica, Melissa and Michelle, remain the ongoing source of utter joy and bliss for me. They continue to provide wisdom, encouragement, unconditional love and plenty of hugs. Thank you, dear ones, for our late night phone calls when I am on the road, for your cards and notes, and for the incredible privilege of being your mother.

My husband Jim continues to believe in me, applaud my every effort and remain steadfast and loyal in the midst of what is sometimes a long-distance relationship. His belief in me is the fuel that has supplied me in some very dark hours. He is a rock, physically and emotionally, an anchor in the sometimes billowing sea of life!

My mother, at 88, still cruises around town delivering her sense of humor to all who know her. She continues to demonstrate the integrity and elevated values that she modeled always for me and my three brothers. Thank you, Mom, for following your clear calling in life as a parent.

My brothers are three of the most wonderful men I ever hope to know in a lifetime. The laughter and dreams we continue to share are treasures in my daily experience.

My deep gratitude and appreciation extend to all my friends in the National Speakers Association who continue to share their wisdom, love and practical advice with me. A huge thank you to my dear, dear friend Liz Curtis Higgs who believes I am called to write and loved me into doing so; and to Jack Canfield and Mark Victor Hansen for including my story in *Chicken Soup for the Soul* which led me to my publisher, Health Communications, Inc.; and to Sam Horn in Hawaii who opened the door to the Maui Writers Conference for me; to Greg Godek who continues to share his own wealth of knowledge about writing; to Cathy Fyock who coached me while on an airplane and believed I could write; to Dan Poynter who sat with me over a long lunch and shared his incredible understanding of the world of writing and publishing.

The person who rescued me in the midst of this manuscript is my friend and wizard on the computer keyboard, Lynn Carlton. Lynn's love, hard work and wisdom singularly allowed me to meet the publishing deadline. What a gift you are!

I want to thank my editor, Christine Belleris, and Peter Vegso, President, of Health Communications, Inc. Your excitement over this book fueled my own commitment to completion. Thank you for your leadership as well.

Finally, I want to thank my audiences and clients everywhere. It has been in preparing for the opportunity to meet your heart's desires that my own have been fulfilled. I love you all.

BOOK ONE

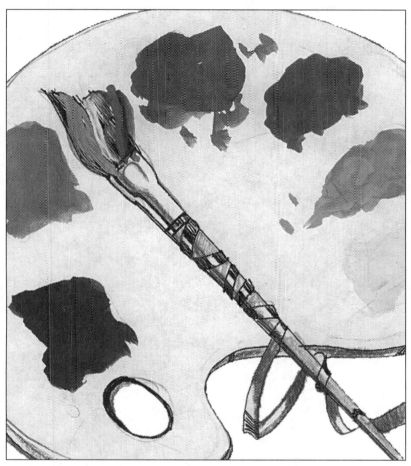

The Foundation for
Your *Fresh Start*

Introduction

Some people might say I have led a storybook life. That doesn't mean I haven't had my hellish experiences. I certainly have! And out of those I have learned much about living a life filled with hope, joy, peace and a multitude of Fresh Starts!

One of the most dramatic *Fresh Starts* came for me on a California freeway when I met the man who was to become my husband. You may have read that story in the *New York Times* bestseller *Chicken Soup for the Soul.* (Read that story in chapter one!)

This book has been created for you if you have a desire to find some practical steps for getting your life together from the inside-out. You will find these pages to be revolutionary if any of these descriptions fit you:

- You would like to get a new grip on your life.
- You have lost your job recently and feel stuck.
- You have a secure job, but you are bored.

- You are in a relationship that isn't working.
- You lack a sense of purpose or meaning in your life.
- You feel somewhat insignificant in the scheme of things.
- You have big dreams and a real sense of purpose but experience the frustration of fear, discouragement, etc.
- You simply have a desire to live a life of peace and serenity.

Whether you are male or female, a business professional or a homemaker, an entrepreneur or a corporate leader, you are most of all a human being with a life. This book is about *your* life, how to live more fully with purpose and meaning.

Revelation and Revolution

Peter Senge, author of *The Fifth Discipline*, makes some interesting observations about the need for a Fresh Start in the corporate world. He makes a clear case for the fact that a revolution in thinking is required. Senge uses the Greek word *metanoia* to describe this revolution:

"[M]etanoia" . . . means a shift of mind. The word has a rich history. For the Greeks, it meant a fundamental shift or change, or more literally transcendence ("meta"—above or beyond, as in "metaphysics") of mind ("noia," from the root "nous," of mind). In the early (Gnostic) Christian tradition, it took on a special meaning of awakening shared intuition and direct knowing of the highest, of God. "Metanoia" was probably the key term of such early Christians as John the Baptist. In the Catholic corpus the word metanoia was eventually translated as "repent."

To grasp the meaning of "metanoia" is to grasp the deeper meaning of "learning," for learning also involves a fundamental shift or movement of mind. [1]

Metanoia is not a form of self-help. It is the result of revelation. It produces life lived from a transformed mind, a totally new point of view.

Probably you have experienced the bumpy road of trying to get your life together. You may even have had some short-term success. But eventually failure, discouragement, and even brick walls seem to show up again. (You will see how and why that happens in a later chapter.) In the words of Christ, "The spirit is willing but the flesh is weak."[2] What you need is an entirely new way of seeing your life.

This book is designed to help you uncover the core of who you are meant to be: the *real you* is *spirit*. You will be relieved to discover how to live your life from your spirit, from the inside-out.

A Philosophical Moment

You know that New Year's resolutions almost never produce lasting change. In fact, we all joke about our resolutions, don't we? Here is an exercise that will be very helpful in preparing you for a Fresh Start!

Take a deep breath, relax and fill in this sentence with all the thoughts that come into your mind.

In my opinion, the reason most New Year's resolutions do not last is because:

---

1. Peter Senge, *The Fifth Discipline* (New York: Doubleday/Currency, 1990), 13.
2. Matt. 26:41.

_____

_____

and because:

_____

_____

Any other thoughts?

_____

_____

I wish I could know exactly what you wrote. It would be invigorating to discuss your thoughts. But, let me share with you what I would have written.

In my opinion, the reason most New Year's resolutions do not last is because:

- Resolutions usually are designed to fix or improve a surface problem or concern or habit in our life without looking at the root cause of our dissatisfaction.

and because:

- We have so many stresses and preoccupations in our lives that we do not have the energy to sustain our commitments or resolutions.

Any other thoughts?

- Most people have never taken the time to discover the foundation of who they are. Resolutions have to be congruent with who we really are in order to bring lasting value and thus be sustained and maintained. This involves revelation.

I find that most people usually are focused on their problems or unhappiness. Many of them think they will be happy as soon as they can get rid of or solve their current problems or change their present condition.

Perhaps you know people who say things like:

- As soon as I get married I'll be happy . . .
- As soon as I get out of this marriage I'll be happy . . .
- When I graduate and get a good job I'll be happy . . .
- As soon as I can get a better job I'll be happy . . .
- When I retire I'm really going to be happy . . .
- As soon as my children grow up and are on their own . . .
- As soon as we can have children then . . .

It's sad, but very often true, that this becomes the on-going saga of some people's lives. *The Art of the Fresh Start* is a book designed to help you discover a life that works today, tomorrow and 20 years from now.

Life-Changing Benefits for You

Many of us read books, listen to speakers and attempt to do what the latest guru suggests as a formula for living. However, like failed New Year's resolutions, usually we face the same frustrations again.

This book is designed to show you how to live out of your own inner sense of wholeness. There are four major, life-long benefits for you hidden in these pages. They are:

Benefit One: You will learn how to determine the unique person you are.

Benefit Two: You will gain the principles and skills to access the *real you*, who you are in your spirit.

Benefit Three: You will become one of those rare people who understands your uniqueness and your purpose. You will be equipped to make resolutions, choices, decisions and commitments that will **endure** because they spring from the real you.

Benefit Four: You will find the **energy** to sustain your commitments because they are **congruent** with the awesome uniqueness with which you have been created.

Come with me on the journey. This is the beginning of a lifetime full to the brim with renewing **Fresh Starts** for you.

Let's begin!

CHAPTER 1

Unique Dreams Have Been Planted in Your Heart!

I learned about miracles when I was 21 years old. But I learned about hope from the time I was born. My father always had a sense of great expectation. He saw life as a series of new opportunities to grow, to change and to experience renewed joy and excitement.

My dad learned to live with hope by having to look into the abyss of hopelessness. In Dale Carnegie's book *How to Stop Worrying and Start Living*, my father, G. A. Arnold, describes his trip to the edge of the Illinois River where he contemplated suicide. He had lost his job and felt like a total failure as a husband and father. A still, small voice told him he could dream and his life would have purpose.[1]

---

1. Dale Carnegie, *How to Stop Worrying and Start Living* (New York: Pocket Books, 1985), 207-208.

He described his inner feelings, "I immediately felt a peace of mind I hadn't known in months."

Out of hopelessness my father experienced a Fresh Start. Later he wrote, "As I look back, I am glad now that I lost everything . . . that tragedy taught me to rely on God." Perhaps it was my father's influence initially that caused me to hear words of hope when, as a young mother, I experienced divorce and a sense of complete personal failure.

In 1977 I was a single mother with three young daughters, a house payment, a car payment and a need to rekindle some dreams.

One evening I attended a seminar and heard a man speak on the I x V = R Principle. (Imagination mixed with Vividness becomes Reality.) The speaker pointed out that the mind thinks in pictures, not in words, and as we vividly picture in our mind what we desire, it will become a reality.

This concept struck a creative chord in my heart. I knew the Biblical truth, that the Lord gives us "the desires of our heart"[2] and that "as a man thinketh in his heart, so is he"[3] I was determined to take my written prayer list and turn it into pictures. I began cutting up old magazines and gathering pictures that depicted the "desires of my heart." I arranged them in an expensive photo album and waited expectantly.

I was very specific with my pictures. They included:

1. A good-looking man.

2. A woman in a wedding gown and a man in a tuxedo.

3. Bouquets of flowers (I'm a romantic).

4. Beautiful diamond jewelry (I rationalized that God

---

2. Ps. 37:4.
3. Prov. 23:7.

loved David and Solomon and they were two of the richest men who ever lived!).

5. An island in the sparkling blue Caribbean.

6. A lovely home.

7. A woman who had recently become vice-president of a large corporation. (I was working for a company that had no female officers. I wanted to be the first woman vice-president in that company.)

About eight weeks later, I was driving down a California freeway minding my own business at 10:30 in the morning. Suddenly a gorgeous red and white Cadillac passed me. I looked at the car because it was a beautiful car. And the driver looked at me and smiled, and I smiled back because I always smile. Now I was in deep trouble. Have you ever done that? I tried to pretend that I hadn't looked. "Who me? I didn't look at you!" He followed me for the next 15 miles. Scared me to death. I drove a few miles, he drove a few miles. I parked, he parked . . . and eventually, I married him!

On the first day after our first date, Jim sent me a dozen roses. Then I found out that he had a hobby. His hobby was collecting diamonds. Big ones! And he was looking for somebody to decorate. I volunteered! We dated for about two years and every Monday morning I received a long-stemmed red rose and a love note from him.

About three months before we were getting married, Jim said to me, "I have found the perfect place to go on our honeymoon. We will go to St. John's Island down in the Caribbean." I laughingly said, "I never would have thought of that!"[4]

---

4. Jack Canfield and Mark Victor Hansen, *Chicken Soup for the Soul* (Deerfield Beach: Health Communication, Inc., 1993), 188-189.

These life-changing events provided me with a practical pattern for living the life that my Creator designed for me to live. This life experience—filled with adventure, peace, serendipities, joy, fun, purpose—is one that allows each day to be a fresh beginning.

We tend to get in a rut, don't we? We fall into a routine that becomes boring. We lose the awareness of our dreams.

After I had been married to Jim for eight years and had been speaking and traveling without much of a vacation, I felt the need to dream again. I felt that I was beginning to get boring. So I said to Jim, "Let's go do something exciting because I talk to people about expanding their horizons and I'm ready for some big dreams."

He said, "What do you want to do?"

I said, "Let's go gorilla tracking in Zaire!"

We created a picture book of Africa. Within six months we met good friends who wanted to know if we would ever consider going to Africa and visiting Dian Fossey's gorillas? We were ready!

That trip was amazing. We flew into Rwanda and drove over into Zaire. We went out to a tiny little park at the foot of the mountains and attended a gorilla workshop! A Twa pygmy explained to us what to do if we ran into the male silverback gorilla.

There were six of us lined up single file for the tracking. Our Twa guide explained, "One thing you need to know: if the male silverback shows up, he will average six to seven feet tall, and weigh 600-700 pounds. He will appear instantly, screaming and beating his chest. The one thing you must not do is run. Instead, drop to the ground, lower your eyes and eat grass."

So, we began our adventure. After we'd been out about two and a half hours, sweating and climbing through the jungle, trying not to step on any safari ants, we heard a wild scream. A gigantic 700-pound silverback showed up, beating his chest! His head appeared to be two feet tall and a foot wide! We stood still, lowered our eyes, sank to the ground and ate grass!

Mushamuka was his name. He brought eight wives and 22 children with him. We sat down and they sat down! The gorillas looked at us, examining us carefully. We were close enough to touch them. It was a phenomenal experience that left me humbled and awed, and it certainly expanded my horizons. Afterward, I reflected on the experience and concluded that, in a world with so much to know and learn and with so many places to go and people to see, how could anyone be bored or depressed?

Sovereign Circumstances

I sat watching Jim make his way through the tables to the lectern. He is not a public speaker, but he had prepared this evenings' speech in his mind for decades. This evening held the fruition of his heart's desire.

Jim was being inducted into the UCLA Hall of Fame as the most outstanding guard to play football for the Bruins in 52 years. He stood tall as he spoke, his words hesitant because of the emotion he felt. His dream had become a reality. One of the major setbacks in Jim's life came to him in second grade. Because of his lack of reading skills and severe dyslexia he could not go on to the third grade with the rest of his class. As a child he was embarrassed and disappointed.

However, this extra year of age and growth was a huge factor in God's plan for fulfilling His plans in Jim's life. By the time he was a senior at Hamilton High School in Los Angeles Jim's size and ability qualified him for a full-ride football scholarship to the University of California at Los

Angeles. His dyslexia was a gigantic blessing and one of the key elements used to fulfill the desires planted in his heart.

Jim Salsbury became an All-American at UCLA and was the number two draft choice for the Detroit Lions in 1955. He played professional ball for both the Detroit Lions and the Green Bay Packers.

Circumstances, even negative circumstances, can provide the clues to what your purpose in life or calling may be. Rather than focus on the surface concerns, soul issues, it is important to observe how the elements of your life work together to bring you to the fulfillment of your heart's desire! My husband, Jim, experienced this reality over a period of decades. Time is an important feature in the fulfillment of the Creator's plan in our lives.

The following pages are filled with insights and practical suggestions designed to trigger your own inner awareness and to stimulate your own sense of purpose.

CHAPTER 2

Your Disgust
Often Precedes the
Discovery of Your Dreams

This is it! You are longing to make a change. Hang on to your feelings. On a scale of 1 to 10, how important is it to you to get a grip on your life?

Fill in your number: _____

Don't think for even a moment about *how* you are going to accomplish this. That thinking process is part of the reason you haven't been able to make the changes before now. Just focus on how very much you need or want to make a change.

You are about to embark on a revolutionary experience that will free you to be who you really are, the unique person the Creator has designed you to be.

15

Before a highway construction company begins building a superhighway, they bring in surveyors to determine the lay of the land and the needs of the project. You, too, need to get a fix on precisely where you are and where you want to be, or don't want to be, before you begin.

Notice what I just said. At this point your survey may show you only where you don't want to be. Don't worry. You will soon learn some techniques for discovering what your hidden hopes and dreams are.

Your Life Survey

So, take a few moments and do a survey of your life as it is right now. Isolate two areas from the list below that you are currently disgusted with about yourself or your own life experience.

___ My Weight   ___ Boredom

___ A Personal Relationship   ___ Hopelessness, Depression

___ My Job   ___ Problems With Children

___ Lack of Money   ___ Worry, Anxiety

___ Drugs, Alcohol Abuse   ___ Fear of Death

___ Purposelessness   ___ Health Problems

What else that isn't listed?

_____   _____

Now prioritize these two areas. Which one is driving you the craziest, or creating the most stress or fear or unhappiness or disruption in your life?

The next exercise holds the secret that is the core element for *The Art of the Fresh Start*. Bring your entire person to this exercise.

Practical Preparation

- Sit in a comfortable chair.
- Be sure your feet are firmly on the floor.
- Take a very deep, full breath through your nose.
- Exhale through your mouth. Totally force out the last bits of breath.
- Repeat that process once or twice more. This will help cleanse your body of toxins and release tension.

Be aware of your spirit, the inner you that is beyond your body and your soul. This graphic may help you sense the location of your spirit:

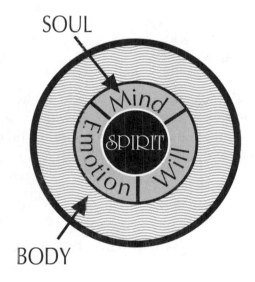

While you are quiet and at rest you may experience additional clarity about what you want to change in your life.

Listening to Your Spirit

There may be many reasons why you want to make changes in your life. Some are usually negative reasons and some are positive.

For example you might say, "I want to lose 25 pounds because . . ."

Negative Reasons:	Positive Reasons:
I feel horrible in my clothes.	I'd like to be attractive.
I look ugly.	My health would improve.
I feel terrible and have no energy	I'd like myself better.
I can't stand to get dressed in the morning.	I'd feel so great in blue jeans.

Begin to focus only on what you really want. Deep inside you is a vision, an image of how the real you prefers to be. Tap into that center within you. Respond to the statements below with all the thoughts and feelings that come to you.

Your statement: "I want to _____ because":

Negative reasons why you are disgusted with this area of your life:

_____

_____

_____

READER/CUSTOMER CARE SURVEY

If you are enjoying this book, please help us serve you better and meet your changing needs by taking a few minutes to complete this survey. Please fold it & drop it in the mail.

As a thank you, we will send you a gift.

Name: _____

Address: _____

_____

Tel. # _____

Gender: ____ Female ____ Male

Age: ____ 18-25 ____ 46-55
____ 26-35 ____ 56-65
____ 36-45 ____ 65+

Marital Status: ____ Married ____ Single
____ Divorced ____ Partner

Is this book: ____ Purchased for self?
____ Purchased for others?
____ Received as gift?

How did you find out about this book?

____ Catalog
____ Store Display
Newspaper
____ Best Seller List
____ Article/Book Review
____ Advertisement
Magazine
____ Feature Article
____ Book Review
____ Advertisement
____ Word of Mouth
____ T.V./Talk Show (Specify) _____
____ Radio/Talk Show (Specify) _____
____ Professional Referral _____
____ Other (Specify) _____

What subject areas do you enjoy reading most? (Rank in order of enjoyment)

____ Women's Issues ____ New Age
____ Business Self Help ____ Aging
____ Relationships ____ Altern. Healing
____ Inspiration ____ Parenting
____ Soul/Spirituality ____ Diet/Nutrition
____ Recovery ____ Exercise/Health
____ Other (Specify) _____

What do you look for when choosing a personal growth book? (Rank in order of importance)

____ Subject ____ Author
____ Title ____ Price
____ Cover Design ____ In Store Location
____ Other (Specify) _____

When do you buy books? (Rank in order of importance)

____ Xmas ____ Father's Day
____ Valentines Day ____ Summer Reading
____ Birthday ____ Thanksgiving
____ Mother's Day
____ Other (Specify) _____

Where do you buy your books? (Rank in order of frequency of purchases)

____ Bookstore ____ Book Club
____ Price Club ____ Mail Order
____ Department Store ____ T.V Shopping
____ Supermarket ____ Airport
____ Health Food Store ____ Drug Store
____ Gift Store ____ Other (Specify)

Additional comments you would like to make to help us serve you better.

_____

_____

_____

3642/273

Thank You !!

FOLD HERE

BUSINESS REPLY MAIL

FIRST CLASS MAIL PERMIT NO 45 DEERFIELD BEACH, FL

POSTAGE WILL BE PAID BY ADDRESSEE

HEALTH COMMUNICATIONS
3201 SW 15TH STREET
DEERFIELD BEACH, FL 33442-9875

Positive reasons why you know you want a Fresh Start:

_____

_____

_____

A Philosophical Moment

- What would you say to your best friend who was considering making some changes?

_____

_____

Genuine desire to change initially springs out of disgust with your body-life or your soul-life. Then comes the awareness of all the positive uniqueness that makes up who you are!

CHAPTER 3

Radical Revelation Creates a Decision to Change

The Psalmist says, "God has given us the desires of our heart."[1] These stirrings in your heart to begin anew are a bubbling up of the unique person God has designed you to be.

Now stick with me. This next truth, about getting on track with your life, is something you haven't heard about before. Consider the illustration again:

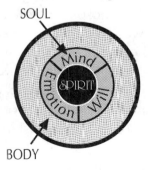

SOUL

Mind

SPIRIT

Emotion

Will

BODY

---

1. Ps. 37:4.

The invisible you is your spirit. This is the real you. This is the essence of you. But you live in a body that interacts with the visible world through your soul, i.e., your mind, your will, your emotions. Herein lies the dilemma that produces the frustration, depression, hopelessness and anguish of broken resolutions and a wasted life.

Let me say it another way. Your mind convinces the real you that it, your mind, is you. No-o-o! You are in charge of your mind. You can be involved in the transformation of your mind so that it conforms to who you are in your spirit! You, the real you, need to go *out* of your mind!

A Living Example

This does not mean that your body and your soul (mind, emotions, will) are not important elements. Rather your body and soul need to be congruent with your spirit, and not limit the full expression of the true you. Let me give you an example of what I mean.

Many years ago I visited Father Damien de Veuster's leper colony on the Hawaiian island of Molokai. The residents' leprosy—a horrible disease that severely disfigures and eventually paralyzes its victims—had been arrested with sulfa drugs. The community functioned normally despite its residents' disfigurement.

One day I visited the hospital cardiac ward. As soon as I entered the ward, I was greeted by a cheery voice. I turned in the direction of the first bed where lay a grotesquely disfigured patient. That was Julie, an 85-year-old survivor of leprosy and a recent heart attack who was without nose, ears, lips, eyelids, arms and legs, but not without her spirit.

"How long will you be on the island?" said the voice that held a smile.

"Only one day," I responded, trying to match her example.

"Then you need to see the children. We're doing fine

here. Thanks for coming by."

In spite of the destruction of her body, Julie spoke from her spirit and our exchange had been heart-lifting. If she had focused on her external circumstances, surely she would have been depressed. Instead she allowed her spirit to bubble up to transform her mind. She accepted her physical limitations and lived from the inside out, whole in spirit, soul and body, and sharing her wholeness.

The Cycle of Chaos

Hugh Prather, in his book *Notes to Myself* said, "To listen to my intuition is to identify with my awareness, to be my entire experience, and not just my conscious perception. . . . When I favor my conscious perception over my total awareness, I can no longer hear the guiding rhythm of one whole reality."[2] See if you agree with this observation.

When you have an overwhelming sense of disgust or frustration and a gigantic desire to change your life for the better, what is the next thing that happens?

Your mind begins to tell you all the reasons why you will not be able to execute your plan, or your mind recounts all of the losses you will incur if you make these changes. And then what happens next?

Fear sets in. Your emotions are now captured and they begin to work against you. Your will to change begins dissipating.

Is this a familiar cycle to you? This is why New Year's resolutions don't work for people who don't understand these revolutionary principles. The normal human experience is to be paralyzed by the logic or the fear. The mind berates you at every turn.

---

2. Hugh Prather, *Notes to Myself* (New York: Bantam Books, 1990).

Let me be sure you can see what is happening. Look back at the graphic on page 21 again. Notice that the mind, emotions and will are interlocking parts of your soul. This interface is designed as a means for us to function in the visible world.

If your mind gives you reasons why you cannot change, your emotions and will are infected. The same is true if your emotions start to send feelings of fear to you. Your mind and will are tied into this chaos. And if your will resists change, (for example, you eat the chocolate cake. Oops!) your mind accuses you, charging that you are undisciplined, weak and hopeless. Of course this depresses you (emotions) and you eat more chocolate cake to prove that you are the loser your mind says you are!

One of my favorite writers describes this experience. "For the good that I would, I do not; but the evil which I would not, that I do . . . Who will deliver me from the body of this death?"[3] This is the human condition. It is the condition that produces the depression, frustration and hopelessness that pull us back into the pit of despair.

The Lazarus Analogy

You may recall the biblical account of Lazarus, the brother of Mary and Martha, who became sick and died. According to the Gospel of John, Lazarus was wrapped in grave clothes, like a mummy, and buried in a cave. A heavy stone was rolled in front of the opening to the cave.

Jesus came to the home of this family four days after Lazarus died. He asked that the stone be removed and Martha objected. "Lord, by this time he stinketh; for he hath been dead four days."[4]

---

3. Rom 7:19, 24b.
4. John 11:13.

Time Out for the Application!

You may have experienced a kind of sickness unto death in your own life. This is that cycle of chaos in the mind. The signs of this living death include boredom, disgust and a feeling of lifelessness.

In fact, you may be whining and complaining to your friends to the point that you qualify for the "he stinketh" description! You might even identify with the darkness and isolation of the cave where Lazarus' body was laid. You may feel bound hand and foot with grave clothes when you consider how to find vitality and purpose in your daily experience. You may feel trapped and lifeless.

The Call to Life

The account of Lazarus' experience continues with Jesus standing before the cave and crying out "Lazarus, come forth."

Imagine: A dead man, wrapped in mummy clothes, rotting for four days, gets a wake-up call!

Question: Could dead Lazarus in his decaying condition have heard the call?

Answer: The answer, of course, is NO!

Question: What had to happen before Lazarus could hear and respond?

Answer: He had to be brought to life by the Creator of Life before he had the ability to hear the call!

Time Out for the Application!

This is the revolutionary truth inherent in *The Art of the Fresh Start:*

> *The human spirit is not adequate to sustain true Life. The human spirit must be touched by the Spirit of Life, God Himself. This new creation is then able to answer the call to come out of the cave and be set free.*

Lazarus is a picture of the powerlessness of a human being who has not experienced God's gift of Life. The power of the Creator lifted Lazarus out of his helpless state! Lazarus came out of the tomb, and, with the help of his friends and family, he disentangled himself from the rags in which he was bound.

This reality may at first seem very disconcerting. Most of us have lived our lives from the humanistic philosophy which says that self-effort, discipline and goal-setting will rescue us from our depression or failures or career setbacks. The idea that we cannot rescue ourselves seems completely ridiculous!

But this reality is the Good News! There is a Life that is not subject to the daily, changing, unpredictable environment in which we exist. This Life has infinite power and has created you and me to live with purpose, infused with His power.

This Life in us frees us to walk out of our darkness and into the Light. This is the life experience which supplies us with purpose, peace and the power to live more balanced and consistent lives.

Your Decision to Change

Let's review the Lazarus lesson as it applies to change. What happened to Lazarus before he decided to get up and walk out of his "cave condition"? He was brought to Life by the Author of Life and then the most natural decision in the world was for Lazarus to decide to get out of his circumstances! And, he was empowered to change! Lazarus experienced a Fresh Start! Imagine the difference if a mere human had simply shouted into the cave and chided Lazarus for being so incompetent, inactive and unresponsive!

Or try to picture dead Lazarus practicing self-help techniques. Herein lies the folly of New Year's resolutions and self-help programs. Our human condition, without the Life-giving work and wisdom of God in us, always ends up in a condition of weakness or powerlessness.

WARNING! CAUTION!

Throughout the chapters to follow you will discover practical suggestions for implementing your own Fresh Start. However, without the clear knowledge of the Source of Life and Power these practical suggestions might only serve to perpetuate your soul-life. Perhaps you want to pause before proceeding and prepare more fully for your Fresh Start.[5]

Spirit Preparation

- Sit in a comfortable place.
- Relax. Breathe. Be still.
- Ask the One who created you to bring His Life to your spirit.
- Remember to say "Thank You."

---

5. See Appendix I on page 169 for an in-depth discussion of the body, soul and spirit relationship.

CHAPTER 4

A Transformed Mind Is the Source of Wise Decisions!

One of life's greatest challenges is making good decisions. The primary reason for this is that chaotic mind we have been discussing. How many times have you said or thought, "I just can't see clearly what I should do." Or, "I know I should probably go back to school and get an MBA but I con't have the money right now." Or, "We should probably buy a home while interest rates are low but I don't know if I am going to keep my job. The company is laying off people." And so it goes, on and on.

The Art of the Fresh Start will teach you to make decisions that will launch you into your desired career, or give you the courage to leave an abusive relationship, or allow you to overcome the fear of going back to college, etc. To achieve clarity and experience the power to make these Fresh Start decisions, you have to find a way to escape your soul-life cycle of chaos.

The Transformation Process

In the world of electric power, the transformer can change the degree and quality of power moving from one point to another. The transformed mind is one that no longer functions like the mind found in "normal" humans! This was one of the discoveries of the Apostle Paul after his spirit was transformed. Paul writes, "Be not conformed to this world but be ye transformed by the renewing of your mind."[1]

It is interesting to note that the Greek word translated "world" actually means "age." In other words, Paul suggests that we not be conformed to this age. You and I live in an age that has almost deified the human mind. The mind has become the source for answers, for values, for wisdom.

Paul, on the other hand, says you and I can actually be transformed (experience an authentic Fresh Start) through the renewing of our mind. This is the *"metanoia"* about which Peter Senge writes.

The renewed mind, therefore, is one that is influenced by the Spirit of God. The Spirit works within you and lifts your mind above the endless soul cycle.[2]

The Role of Faith

Making decisions with a renewed mind involves believing that the Spirit of God is at work in you. Faith is the invisible awareness that your decisions and direction are being supplied by the Creator. You then can move to the practical process because your renewed mind is not counting on itself for wisdom.

---

1. Rom. 12:2b.
2. See Appendix II on page 171 for an in-depth discussion of the mind.

The AAA$_{bc}$ Formula

You will remember that your emotions are a part of your soul-life. It is impossible to separate the mind, emotions and will. When you make a decision, your emotions play a part in the process. Your "renewed emotions" are very sensitive to what produces a sense of peace within you and what elicits a kind of uneasiness. In every difficult decision your mind and emotions are really considering only three options.

Here are your options. (I call this the Triple A,b,c Formula for engineering your Fresh Start.)

ALTER
AVOID
ACCEPT
>   *build your strength (emotionally, physically, spiritually).*
>   *change your perspective.*

To illustrate, if you are disgusted with your weight and you want to create a change in your body you can:

ALTER the amount and kind of food you eat.
or
AVOID food altogether.
or
ACCEPT the fact that you will always be the size you are, so:
build your strength by seeing your other gifts and talents.
change your perspective about the importance of your body size.

Let's use another more gripping example. Suppose you are in an abusive or unhealthy relationship. You have three options:

ALTER *the relationship through counseling or other behavioral changes.*

or

AVOID *the situation completely by removing yourself from it.*

or

ACCEPT *the situation for the moment. This means you must:*

> **b**uild *your strength by participating in a weekly support group. Actively fill your mind with encouraging ideas and focus attention on the blessings in your life.*
>
> **c**hange *your perspective by setting a time limit on the situation.*

One last example. If you are facing a career decision you have only one of these options. You can:

ALTER *your current work experience by changing departments or, if you are unemployed, by considering a completely different field.*

AVOID *your current work experience, perhaps by resigning.*

ACCEPT *your current situation because the financial risk is too great to warrant quitting at this time.* **b**uild *your strength by developing other passions.* **c**hange *your perspective by planning your next career, and have a timeline in mind.*

Your Personal Clarity

Let's review your commitment to change and your disgust or frustration with the current circumstance or issue in your life. Restate what the inner you is saying:

"I want to _____

because _____."

Now, hang on. You are going to outfox your chaotic mind! The real you (spirit) is not a victim of circumstances because the real you has desires planted deep within that have been ordained for you. Which is your option of choice for executing the Fresh Start in your life?

> *Will you **ALTER** your actions or situation?*
>> *or*
> *Will you **AVOID** your circumstances?*
>> *or*
> *Will you **ACCEPT** and make adjustments in other areas?*

Using an active sense of faith check your spirit as you consider each of the options. As you picture each alternative which one provides you with the greatest sense of *peace?* Do you have a greater sense of relief with one option in particular? Does one option give you a greater sense of inner joy or excitement?

Your spirit is the real you responding to the prompting of the wisdom of God. God does not give you a spirit of fear, but rather provides you with a feeling of empowerment, a sense of being loved, and clarity of thought

Finally, this AAA_{bc} Formula quiets your chaotic mind and allows the real you to consider options based on your values and the dreams hidden in your heart. You will actually begin to experience glimmers of feelings of renewed hope!

Your Clear Vision

You are going to apply these principles in many areas of your life. Your energy and enthusiasm for growth and change will be fueled by the euphoria springing up in your spirit. For now, however, you want to have a single focus, a clear vision of your future in one specific arena.

Once again repeat the exercise of bringing yourself fully into this present moment.

- Feet on the floor.
- Deep, full breath through your nose.
- Completely exhale through your mouth.
- Conscious awareness of the inner you.

Now, write a statement that reflects your decision. Use as many exciting or descriptive words as might be appropriate.

> EX: I want to say good-bye to this stale, unproductive relationship in my life because I know that God has called me to higher and better things.

> EX: I have decided to avoid this relationship permanently because I want to fill my life with meaningful, productive activities.

Your Statements

"I want to _____

because _____."

"I have decided to _____

because _____."

A True Story

I remember her well: long blonde hair, natural beauty, no make-up, sparkling blue eyes. She worked for a large Fortune 500 company and she was participating in one of my seminars on team-building. Her name was Cindy[3] and she was annoyed, rebellious, defensive and unhappy.

"You're talking about building relationships," Cindy complained. "The people I work with are selfish, negative and only interested in corporate politics. I hate this job." Obviously Cindy needed to make a change.

One potential solution to Cindy's dilemma might have been for her to make a resolution to be friendlier with her colleagues and less judgmental. Maybe she needed to decide to become a team player. Do you think that would have worked for Cindy? I wasn't sure it would, so I suggested that Cindy and I look at the AAA_{bc} formula. We reviewed her options together. She could **alter** her relationships by changing her behavior. She might need to **avoid** her unhappiness by quitting, or she could **accept** the miserable career experience and try to cope (b,c). I asked her which felt most freeing in her spirit. She instantly selected option number two—**avoiding** the situation produced the most peace for her. But then fear grabbed her mind.

"I need this job. I have bills. How can I quit?"

I asked this attractive 28-year-old the dream question. "If you could do anything with your life, what would it be?"

Her face broke into a smile that contained glimmers of genuine joy. In a steady, full voice she replied, "I would work with animals, not as a vet, but as an animal trainer. I especially love dolphins."

---

3. Not her real name.

There was no place for Cindy to do that in Norwalk, Connecticut. But she selected her option, got focused on her dream and within one year Cindy was working at Sea World feeding the dolphins.

Cindy made a decision based on her disgust for her situation and her desire to make a change. She touched her spirit's joy when she heard her own answer to the dream question. Her excitement and sense of hope gave her the energy to act, the AAA_{bc} Formula gave her the clarity to act, and Cindy experienced *The Art of the Fresh Start!*

"You are where you are because you have not taken yourself somewhere else." I don't know who said that, but there is truth to it. Many people today have not experienced a renewed mind, so they spend years blaming their childhood experiences, or their company, or their spouse for their difficult circumstances. That sense of being the victim leads to powerlessness and paralysis. People can be trapped in that mentality and cannot bring themselves to a Fresh Start.

A Crucial Truth

If you sense that you have a victim attitude, let me encourage you with a crucial truth:

> *You are where you are because you would rather be there for now. And that is perfect for you for now. Remember, change involves responding to the true desire of your heart.*

> *For now be sure to embrace where you are. Say to yourself, aloud, "I prefer to be where I am as I am for now. This is the life I prefer to live now. When I want to be somewhere else or experience some other emotion, I will."*

The very act of saying this aloud will move you out of your chaotic mind. A Fresh Start will come more easily as you see your current condition more clearly.

Clarity, Focus, Energy

The inherent value in the AAA_{bc} Formula is the clarity that begins to come to you—from the inside-out. This clarity is accompanied by the focus and energy needed to act. This is how lasting commitments are achieved.

CHAPTER 5

Clues to the Real You Are Hidden in Your Personal Preferences, Priorities and Values

Have you ever stood on the rim of the Grand Canyon and experienced the physical, emotional sensation of that marvel? Perhaps you have skied on perfect, fresh, powdery snow on the ridge of a breathtaking mountain with crystal blue sky overhead. What moment in your life experiences captures your whole being in awesomeness? Write it down and relive your feelings for a moment.

_____

_____

Did you have some sense of the miraculous or perhaps feel euphoric about your life in that moment?

Seeing into your own amazing uniqueness can produce these same feelings. I remember exactly where I was sitting and what I was doing when I first glimpsed the life-changing revelation about the uniqueness of values in our individual lives.

A True Story

Monica, my oldest daughter, had just graduated from UCLA and was interviewing with an outstanding Fortune 500 company. She came home from her third interview in tears. "They're going to offer me a good job and I realize I will hate the job!" she said.

As a parent who thought finding a job was a good idea, I was a little taken aback by her outburst. I poured us a couple of glasses of iced tea and we sat down together at the kitchen table. I asked Monica what made her so sure she would not enjoy the position. Her response opened up a Grand Canyon view for me.

"I'm not competitive when it comes to money. This is commission selling with the constant pressure to compete with the rest of the sales team. None of that is important to me. It's not who I am!"

Distinctions! That's it! Who you are is in your spirit. You have preferences, likes and dislikes. Some things in life are important to you. Others are not!

Monica as a person became a fresh object of wonder and curiosity for me. Quietly, with my entire being listening, I asked, "What is important to you? What are those things that you do know you value?"

Thoughtfully she focused on her own inner person. "Well, Mom, I think the most important thing in my life is my family. Also my faith is a critical part of who I am. I need a relatively peaceful lifestyle to nurture my faith and have time for the family."

That was the beginning. Monica and I got pen and paper and began to make a list of each of our unique needs, passions and values. Monica's list contained these elements:

Faith	Control
Family	Peace
Leisure	Love
Structure	Marriage
Security	Children

This list became the basis for Monica's Fresh Start. She began to explore careers that would include these elements. She had the revelation that her choice of where to live was affected by this list, as our family lived in Arizona.

Monica's revelation about herself resulted in her return to school to earn a teaching credential (structure, security, control) Soon after that she met a great guy while sharing a hymn book at church (faith); they are happily married with two little boys and live in Arizona (family, love, marriage, children). Monica is a stay-at-home mom by choice. (For now, less stress, peace, security).

Notice the steps Monica lived through:

1. She became *disgusted* with the direction she was going.
2. She had a radical *revelation* about herself through looking at her own personal values.
3. She used her *transformed mind* to make wise decisions for a new direction.
4. These decisions led her to her *dreams*.

Her dreams became reality. The Creator had hidden these desires in her heart. And note that her desires are congruent with, and emerged from, her values.

A Moment for You to Ponder

Has Monica's story triggered any thoughts in you? Maybe you are saying, "She'd have made a lot more money in sales!" Or, "Teaching would be boring for me." Or, "I wouldn't want to live that close to my family. I like my independence."

The insights or feelings you may have had about your own values and preferences are huge clues for creating a new beginning in your life!

Write down some of your key values or passions. These will be elements critical to your sense of well-being, and your sense of joy and satisfaction.

Another True Story

Melissa, my second oldest daughter, graduated from UCLA and worked in California for more than a year after graduation. One Tuesday morning I answered the phone and an anguished voice I barely recognized said, "Mom, I need to come home this weekend and rethink my life. I am stressed to the max."

Time-Out for a Clue

One of the major signals for considering a Fresh Start in your life is negative stress. You have been designed to utilize stress as a positive motivator in your life. If you are living a life you love, it is the positive stress (eustress) of excitement or enthusiasm that gives you energy and strength.

When the effects of stress produce depression, illness, frustration, irritation, etc., you are being given strong signals. You are experiencing incongruity. In other words, somewhere in your life your values are being compromised. The unique you, the real you (spirit) is being blocked by outward actions (body) or thoughts (soul) which contradict what is deep inside of you.

For instance, if family or parenting is one of your top two or three passions, you need to have plenty of quality family time. As a working mother who leaves behind a crying child, you will be stressed by your inner incongruity and your outer responsibilities.

Maybe you are a father who is torn between a career that includes long hours and little time for your children, thus compromising your values.

Another Time-Out for You

Without too much soul searching, are you aware of any areas in your current reality that don't fit who you are? Review your work, your habits, your use of time, your relationships. What may be "out of sync" or incongruent for you? (Melissa's phone call was a result of her sense of incongruence.)

Melissa's Revelations

The life-changing Grand Canyon insight I experienced with Monica became valuable for Melissa. She put on paper her personal likes and dislikes. Her values, preferences and personal insights took on incredible clarity for her. Her list included:

Supporting others vs. managing them

Relaxed lifestyle vs. corporate image

Time for fun

Time for family

Helping people

Animals

Spiritual growth

Less pressure, less structure

A few close friends vs. the Friday night T.G.I.F. social scene

Melissa applied the AAA_{bc} principle to her circumstances. Her California career involved managing thirty people in a high-stress sales environment, working sometimes six days a week, dressing to fit the corporate image, and sharing an apartment with friends who were in similar fast-paced jobs. The outlet for everyone had become the Friday night social scene. The positive element was a very good income. She knew the income could not be replaced easily in another endeavor.

What could she **alter** that would solve the negatives?

Was she willing to **avoid** the job, quit and risk the loss of income and security?

Or could she, for the time being **accept** the circumstances, cope with the stress, and enjoy the friends, freedom and money she did have?

Melissa made her Fresh Start choices by examining her feelings when she pictured answers to each of those questions. She still felt bound-up and trapped when she considered **altering** any single element in her life. Changing jobs still left her with a personal lifestyle that felt inappropriate. Changing friends or moving would involve a sense of loneliness and the job stress would remain.

The idea of **accepting** her situation felt impossible. The thought of that option overwhelmed her sense of inner peace. She was faced with **avoiding**, or starting over, what wasn't working.

A Philosophical Moment

You may have strong feelings or thoughts about being a quitter. Perhaps you have a tape playing in your mind saying:

"Other people wouldn't quit in a situation like this. They would probably gut it out—the old no pain, no gain principle. But I am miserable. . . .

"What will other people think if I quit?"

TRUTH: Other people won't think anything. They are so stressed with their own incongruities they don't think about you and your problems.

or

"What will my family, friends, spouse, employer, etc. say?"

TRUTH: These people also are occupied with their own problems, but they are close enough to you to give you opinions and advice. Unfortunately, that can make you feel judged or wrong or inadequate or confused.

or

"I am not a quitter. **Avoidance** is a form of running away from my problems. That won't solve anything."

Do you have any of these thoughts or concerns running through your mind as you consider **avoiding** something or someone in your current reality? Try to identify what old negative tapes your mind is playing. Write out any thoughts you have:

_____

_____

Now consider a fresh look at the **avoidance** option. In order to say yes to one person or project or event in your life you are automatically saying no to other people or activities at that moment. Saying no (**avoidance**) is often the most positive step you can take in order to get to a place of saying yes.

For example, your calendar may be filled with meetings or volunteer work or even golf games. Potentially, you will be missing great, quality family time, or reading time, or a weekend of water skiing. Choosing **avoidance** as an option is often the first step toward making room for congruence with your spirit!

Another Look at the Secret Weapon for Creating a Fresh Start

Once more review the now-familiar circles:

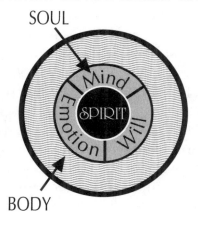

Many times the tapes that play in your mind are the very cause of your feeling trapped, confused, a victim of your circumstances. They can paralyze you and prevent you from risking change.

Recall the fact that *you* are not *your* mind. Your mind is a God-given tool, to be directed and transformed by the work of His spirit in your spirit. This is the secret weapon of genuine, enduring Fresh Starts!

Who you are in your spirit is the you who has power and purpose. This you will burst through the confines of fears, frustrations and worn-out, treadmill mind-patterns.

Melissa's Fresh Start

Change has some challenges. Melissa knew in her spirit what she needed to do. She sensed that **avoidance** was her best option. She had greater peace there. But the practical actions to make it happen required some courage and a huge amount of commitment.

Two elements helped her implement the practical actions:

1. She began to focus on the vision of the specifics of what an ideal life would look like for her.

2. She recognized that her other two options (**alter** or **accept**) were simply unacceptable! This truth required action.

The actual results in Melissa's life included a move home (family) to Arizona while she went back to school to gain computer skills. She was hired on her first interview and is now a senior sales administrator on a great team of people (support role) in an entrepreneurial, small company (more relaxed lifestyle; less structure). She moved into her own apartment, has two cats and rides horses regularly! (Animals.)

Once again this Fresh Start emerged as a result of:

1. **Disgust**—Melissa was stressed out in her current circumstances.
2. **Revelation**—She took time to analyze her values, preferences and passions.
3. **Transformational Thinking**—She made wise decisions which were congruent with her values.
4. **Dreams Becoming Reality**—These choices eventually opened the doors to the dreams that had been planted in Melissa's heart. And her choices were a result of the Creator's renewal process in her life.

A Helpful Aha!

Life is always moving or it wouldn't be *life*. Your goals, values, needs and preferences will change. Your circumstances change: new challenges, new concerns, new opportunities. This is why you want to gain the skills and acquire the knowledge that will equip you for the many moments that will need Fresh Starts.

Meet Michelle

Come with me once more and explore life through the eyes of my third daughter. (You may be glad to know that I have no other children!)

The individuality of gifts, talents, values and preferences often is most evident among siblings. Raised in a similar environment, sharing genetic similarities, having the same role models, yet each has a completely different personality and preferences. This is a common phenomenon.

Many times we try to explain these apparent differences by saying, she's the youngest, he's a middle child, we moved to the city when she was born, and so on. But what is far more important than understanding the why, is simply recognizing your foundation, the unique ingredients from which the real you springs.

Michelle has benefited from observing her two older sisters. When the Grand Canyon revelation came to her in living color, she began early to analyze her values and preferences.

Her palette of life preferences looked like this:

Independence	Change
Freedom	Family
Adventure	Faith
Challenge	Career
Risk	Excitement
Wisdom	Knowledge

Take a moment and refer back to Monica's list and Melissa's list. Observe the commonalities and differences. It becomes clear that there are some values that many people share and consider essential to having a meaningful life. But it is also evident that the differences in people are dramatic.

A Brief Observation

Have you ever wondered why some people value adventure and others value security? Even those in a similar environment, like siblings, have unique preferences. Perhaps this is part of the heart-DNA.

Imagine what Michelle's life experience would have been if she had gotten a degree in education, settled down, taught school and lived a scheduled, structured life. Do you think she might have become stir-crazy? Remember, she prefers adventure, risk and freedom.

Let's suppose she gets stir-crazy, recognizes it and makes a New Year's resolution to create more excitement and adventure in her life. Will she be happy? Will she be satisfied with a trip to the mountains or Manhattan now and then? Probably not! Why? Because the foundational preferences in her life would not be the warp and woof of her everyday experience.

The Good News

The good news for Michelle was her self-awareness. Today she lives in California (independence) and is the regional manager of three upscale Italian restaurants (challenge, freedom, career). Every day she has new experiences with menus, vendors, guests, staff (risk, adventure, knowledge). She visits Arizona when she needs the family experience. Her life unfolds with very little structure, numerous serendipities and a multitude of loose ends! Some people would find that lifestyle far too stressful. (Distress!) It is stressful and that is one of the benefits for Michelle! (Eustress!) As the youngest in the family, she got a head start on her Fresh Start!

It's Your Turn

You may have been quite clear about many of your foundational values and preferences before you read about Monica, Melissa and Michelle. Or, perhaps you are still quite vague about what's important to you. Don't worry. You will have many more tools to uncover your own treasure before we finish this journey.

Just take time out now. Utilize the centering techniques in order to tap into your spirit and bypass your mental gyrations.

- Find a quiet place and a comfortable chair.
- Plant your feet firmly on the floor.

- Take a deep breath through your nose.
- Exhale completely through your mouth.
- Repeat the process.
- Be aware of your spirit, alive in His Spirit!

If prayer is a meaningful part of your life this is a great time to ask the One who created you to provide you with insight and wisdom.

Begin to list at least six or eight values and preferences that you feel make up the unique you.

_____   _____

_____   _____

_____   _____

_____   _____

These are the hidden clues to the real you. These are the spectacular colors on your palette from which you can paint a life full of meaning. They are the colors that have been given to you. And, as in nearly all great art, there is a flow, a congruency that is visible. You are the masterpiece in the analogy.

Here are some additional values for you to consider. Are any of these more significant to you than what you have recorded?

____Money   ____Health

____Recognition   ____Love

____Independence   ____Peace

____Family   ____Challenge

____Faith   ____Excitement

____Structure   ____People

____Time; Punctuality ____Serving others

____Security   ____Fame

____Solitude   ____Orderliness

____Appreciation   ____Beauty

____Power   ____Adventure

____Creativity   ____Cleanliness

____Knowledge   ____Purpose

____Cultural activities ____Ideas; Wisdom

____Competition; Winning ____Others:

_____   _____

_____   _____

_____   _____

_____   _____

Pay attention to your spirit as you create your list. Are there certain values or preferences that kindle a sense of excitement, hope, joy, or curiosity in your spirit? Pay attention to what touches the core of your feelings in a positive, connected way. Your inner response is a good guide to your foundational values.

A More Difficult Assignment
(But Equally Enlightening)

Look over your list and make an attempt to prioritize the six or eight items you have selected. Which one is most important to you? And next?

1. _____

2. _____

3. _____

4. _____

5. _____

6. _____

7. _____

8. _____

This is an arbitrary, outrageous assignment because probably you feel some are equally important and, depending on your circumstances, your priority choices may shift. It doesn't matter. This is an insight opportunity.

Your Insight Opportunity

Consider your current lifestyle and your stated values. On a scale of 1 to 10 (10 being very congruent) how congruent is your life at this time? How well does your life match your values? _____

Look at your priority choices. How well does the time you invest in your life (percent with family, with career, with adventure, etc.) line up with your priority values? _____

Your responses here will give you insight into how much foundation work you decide to do.

Reflection

Remember the comparison of my personal revelation with the view of the Grand Canyon? You may have had some new scenery open up for you during the exercises of this chapter. What revelation or insight or flash of intuitive wisdom has dawned on your spirit?

_____

_____

Others?

_____

_____

_____

_____

Based on these insights what changes, additions or small adjustments would you like to make in your life? Write a few sentences that capture your personal insights and feelings at this moment. You are, remember, moving toward increased congruity.

_____

_____

_____

_____

CHAPTER 6

You Can Bypass Bondage and Leap into Freedom

The Art of the Fresh Start is multi-colored and multi-designed! By that I mean there are innumerable creative actions that will help you establish your solid foundation for living. Using the artist analogy you can choose to paint immediately with bold colors, wild designs and a wide brush; or, you may select pastels and draw with caution and care. It doesn't matter. What does matter is that you begin! Place your brush on your palette and dare to create.

Your desire to start over to build a new life, or simply to change some areas in your life, can meet major pockets of resistance. Before you can be successful in keeping your New Year's resolutions or in creating meaningful change, you will need to pinpoint those pockets of resistance and bondage. Self-sabotage is that dark side of ourselves that prefers misery, martyrdom and meaninglessness. One of your major weapons of warfare is to name the factors that are working against your Fresh Start.

Mental Bondage

Here are a few of the potential enemies that keep you enslaved in mental chaos:

Low Self-Esteem—Your mind says that you really are a nobody. You have made such serious mistakes that you don't deserve to be happy. You aren't smart enough, you're too old, you're not as capable as other people and you simply do not have the capacity to change.

Lack of Energy—Everything looks overwhelming. You feel too tired to go to the gym, or to tell a person the relationship is over, or to go back to school, or work a second job. It seems easier to remain miserable and listless.

In addition, your mind says, "Who cares anyway? I have no real purpose in living so why exert the energy to try to be somebody or to get better."

Depression—Emotionally you are living under a black cloud. You feel trapped with no way out. You feel hopeless. You may even be replaying and rehearsing all the terrible things that have happened to you. You feel like a victim.

No Time—Because time is such a major commodity most of us see it as precious. We will not give up the few moments we have left. When you consider change, your mind cries out, "You don't have time to do this! Your children will suffer, you will have no time to sleep, you'll be exhausted."

Not Enough Money—Many of the major changes you contemplate seem to involve money: join a gym, quit your job, further your education, relocate, etc. Money is one of the preoccupations of our society.

The Fear Factor: Emotional Bondage

Fear of the unknown, fear of change, fear of looking foolish, fear of making a mistake, fear of failing. The list is endless. *Use your fears to fuel your future.* Instead of seeing your fears as chains that make you an emotional cripple, utilize them as guideposts.

For example, if you are afraid to quit your job and move to the Virgin Islands, which may be your secret passion, simply speak to your mind. "Thank you for that little red flag. I must value security (or money) more than I value risk (or adventure) at this moment. I believe I will choose to visit the Virgin Islands for two weeks in April this year."

The Five-Step Plan to Gain Freedom from Your Fears

1. Recognize the fear or concern.
2. Value it instead of fearing it.
3. Keep your forward focus and your vision.
4. Commit to an action that is congruent with your current understanding.
5. Trust the real you—that is faith at work!

This five-step process for dealing with fear will help you again and again. You may want to write out the steps and put them on the dashboard of your car, on your desk, on the bathroom mirror or on your refrigerator. Part of the experience of a renewed, transformed mind is learning to see what is happening in the chaotic mind and transferring it, by faith, to the heavenly perspective!

A Giant Paradox

The truth that I am now going to unveil is so powerful, so life-changing, and so SIMPLE that you may resist it at first. Dare to let go of your preconceived ideas and listen with your spirit.

"THAT WHICH YOU RESIST WILL PERSIST."

A Giant Leap of Faith

To transfer out of the mental chaos, soul-life, caused by this giant paradox requires a giant leap of faith. In other words, you have to take steps that seem unrealistic and illogical! But, look at those two words: unrealistic and illogical. Those are mind words. Consider practicing these faith, spirit-life, principles:

1. *Forget the how.*

Give up all attempts to think through a way to over-come the fears and concerns you have isolated as uniquely yours! Forget it. There are no solutions to these concerns you have. Trying to create a plan paralyzes you. Let the how evolve and surprise you! Insight: One of the reasons you may not have been successful with resolutions or creating change in the past is because you were trying to be logical! When your mind moves into chaos, it is time for you to move into your spirit.

2. *Focus on your willingness.*

Does the following statement ring any inner bells for you?

"I have a deep, powerful desire to change. I am absolutely willing to have positive changes come into my life as they are directed by the Creator who designed me and knows the real me."

Think about your willingness to experience this ideal future. It will emerge from the change you are considering. What does it look like? Use as many colorful, imaginative words as you can to paint this picture of your emerging dreams.

3. **Focus on your future.**

"I am looking forward to taking some baby steps toward my goals as a demonstration of my heartfelt commitment to change."

Do you remember the comical depiction of the psychiatrist and his patient in the movie *What About Bob?* The patient, Bob, seemed to have no sense that he could make any lasting changes. He was advised to take baby steps toward change and, of course, the results were revolutionary, to the dismay of his psychiatrist!

Your third action of faith is to say an emphatic YES in your spirit to the statement above about baby steps. Once again you are not thinking about what these steps might be. Rather you are reinforcing your sense of vision based on faith. A vision, by definition, is a picture of the future that hasn't yet become a reality.

This is a revolutionary insight. When your mind focuses on a problem in order to resist or avoid it, like quitting smoking, the problem grows and fills your mind! The study of psycholinguistics shows that we move toward what we think about. When we focus on our fears and concerns there's no room for the positive.

A Philosophical Moment

Take a few moments to outline the transformational steps we have been discussing. This process will serve you for a lifetime. It contains *The Art of the Fresh Start!*

1. **Isolate the arguments or issues that your chaotic mind uses to sabotage you and to tell you why you can't change or experience your dreams.**
   List these below:

_____

_____

2. **Utilize the Five-Step Plan for facing your fears. (Practice these steps again now.)**

- Name the fear that comes up for you when you consider making a change in your life. (**Recognize the fear or concern.**)

_____

_____

- Say a small thank you for that fear. It is your guidepost to reveal an area in which your faith will work. (**Value the fear.**)
- Create a clear picture of what your life will look like when you are free. (**Forward vision or focus.**)
- Consider a baby step you can take toward your vision. What will it be? (**Action step.**)

_____

_____

(This action step may be as small as putting a physical picture of your vision where you can see it each day.)

- Consciously trust the Spirit at work in you. (**Faith.**)

3. **Write out the three faith principles, using the first person:**

EX: • I will forget the how!

- I _____

- I _____

Summary

Every lasting, meaningful change in your life will be kicked into high gear by faith, not by logic. Stay alert. Begin to observe the miraculous little things that unfold in your life. You will step out of the darkness and into the light. This kind of faith will set you free!

CHAPTER 7

Paint Your Picture by Faith; Calm Your Mind by Breathing

Before you begin the practical baby steps toward change, it will be helpful to gain more insight into the fine art of painting your future. Thomas F. Crum has written a book on *The Magic of Conflict: Turning a Life of Work Into a Work of Art*. As an expert in Aikido, a Japanese martial art, Tom has applied those physical principles to the world of personal and professional choice and change.

Tom teaches that conflict, or negative circumstances and situations, is not viewed as negative by nature. "Nature uses conflict as a primary motivator for change." Tom uses the oyster as an example. As an irritant enters the oyster's world it is embraced and becomes a thing of great value, a pearl. Instead of fighting against an irritant, nature utilizes it as a tool for transformation.[1]

---

1. Thomas F. Crum, *The Magic of Conflict* (New York: Simon and Schuster, 1988), 36.

This is what those fears and concerns we discussed earlier do for you. They serve as the pole to help you vault out of the irritation stage into the action stage of personal growth.

In Tom's use of Aikido, he demonstrates the inner power that is created through a personal centering that flows from clarity of vision and purpose. The forward vision, or clear purpose of a person, provides the physical energy to walk away from those limiting elements that were once a source of conflict. Clarity of vision is one of the key elements in the Fresh Start process. So, how does this reconcile with the principle of faith we just discussed?

Faith Produces Positive Expectations

Faith means that, although you can't see how something will work out, you trust that your vision will become a reality. Thus, you get clear about what you do want and trust that the process will take care of itself. This produces positive expectations.

Remember the story in Chapter One of how I met my husband after creating my picture book of goals? I had no idea how my desires would or could ever become realities. I trusted the One who created me.

Gary and Pat Emery, authors of *The Second Force,* provide further insight into this phenomenon with the diagram on the next page.[2]

---

2. Gary Emery and Pat Emery, *Second Force* (New York: PAL-Dutton, 1990), 166.

WILLINGNESS

WILLFULNESS   **LACK OF WILL**

Most people wear themselves out moving back and forth horizontally between the desire to make positive changes and the fear or lack of ability to make these changes. ("I will . . . I can't. I will . . . I can't.) The Emerys suggest the importance of simple willingness. This is the heavenly atmosphere of faith and high expectations instead of self-effort and failure.

The challenge lies in breaking the bondage of horizontal movement. It's the same kind of crippling bondage that springs from the fears generated in the "what if" questions. How is it possible to utilize this negative state of mind to vault into peace and calm? How do you access the state of willingness that the Emerys illustrate with the triangle?

There are two simple activities for moving out of chaos and fear. First, get very clear about your vision of the ideal elements you desire in your life. Then practice escaping your soul-life through the simple act of conscious breathing.

Breathing: Vital to Building a Life

Life is one breath at a time. The physiological process of breathing is involuntary and mostly unconscious. Yet without breathing we couldn't live. BREATHING IS VITAL!

So, let's take a few moments out and appreciate this miraculous process that allows us to do LESS IMPORTANT ACTIVITIES, physiologically speaking.

We are taking time to observe this process because there are some helpful insights for us to use in the transformational process.

A Life-Giving Exercise

Instructions:

- Be still, very still.
- Shut off the TV or other distractions.
- Center your mind on your rhythmic breathing.
- Consciously breathe in deeply through your nose.
- Exhale through your mouth, fully.
- As you continue to repeat this process, ask these questions:
    - ⇨ How do my toes feel?
    - ⇨ How do my knees feel?
    - ⇨ How do my buttocks feel?
    - ⇨ My back?
    - ⇨ My neck? Shoulders? Arms?
    - ⇨ My inner organs? My heart?
    - ⇨ How does my mind feel?

Observations for your consideration:

- Do you have a slightly greater sense of appreciation for this amazing body as you are quiet?
- Are you experiencing an increased sense of calm and peace as you are aware of rhythmic breathing?
- Do you feel more centered as a person?

- Would you be somewhat less apt to argue, confront or react at this very moment?

A Philosophical Moment

Most people answer yes to these observation questions. The lesson is this: You and I can experience greater peace in our lives as we become quiet and listen to His Presence.

You have just created for yourself some moments of "feel good" or "feel better" through simply becoming conscious and present to the activity of breathing. This activity allows you to listen to the Source of Life!

This is a foundational principle in building a life vs. building a career.

> NOTE: You are not in control of whether your heart suddenly stops and you quit breathing. Thus, the activity is not about control. Rather, it is about appreciation and observation. Ultimately, it is about being awake to your life. In addition, it is about being conscious, present and involved in your moment-by-moment life experience as a person who is being transformed.

The Little Stuff of Life

My friend Rosita Perez is a person who knows how to live creatively. She recounts the "aha" she experienced through her husband Ray's insight. She explains that she was concerned and complaining about a particular situation and Ray finally said to her, "Rosie, do me a favor! Don't sweat the small stuff."

She looked at him with a disdain that only a wife who has been married for many years would dare display and said, "Don't sweat the small stuff? Tell me, what is 'big stuff' to Ray Perez? I want to know!"

He looked at her seriously and said, "Rosie, you really want to know what big stuff is? Big stuff? You're born! Big stuff? You die! Everything in between is little stuff."

Now there's a perspective that supports the importance of breathing! Breath comes at birth, breath leaves at death. So the fact that you are still breathing means you're still alive! The question is, are you living your life or are you really just an animated carcass?

What Is That Smell?

Activity does not necessarily equate to authentic life. For example, have you ever had your nose tell you something was rotting in your kitchen or pantry? You open drawers and cupboards and finally find the culprit in the back of the drawer under the oven. It is a bag of potatoes!

On closer examination, you discover that the potatoes have not been quietly sitting in the drawer—they have been quite active. Thick white, gnarled sprouts are growing from them, and, judging by their size, have been for sometime. The once firm spuds are turning into a putrid pile of mush. Your diagnosis: this is one bag of rotten potatoes!

Observation: Frantic activity can be a major sign of death not life! This "little stuff" all too often becomes "big stuff"!

A Moment for Reflection

The Art of the Fresh Start involves more than making a resolution here or there. It is even more than a single sweeping change in a major area of your life. Rather, *The Art of the Fresh Start* is to learn and utilize concepts, skills, and insights that allow you to create meaningful living for yourself. Every day, in every breath.

So, reflect on the activity in your life. Think about these questions. Then listen intuitively to your answers:

Is there a frenetic, out-of-control feeling to my life?

Do I feel cheated about living because I'm so busy?

Do I feel that, to some degree, I don't have a life?

Do I feel like life is passing me by?

OR

Do I feel a sense of rhythm and balance in the midst of my activity?

Do I feel a sense of fulfillment or satisfaction in my activity?

Even when things are a little crazy, do I feel it is worth the momentary pressure because my activities are really meaningful?

Summarize your overall response to these two sets of questions. Which set most describes your feelings when you answer yes? In two or three sentences describe where you believe you are in your experience of busyness and activity.

_____

_____

_____

_____

If your reflection causes you to see yourself currently as an animated carcass frantically trying to bounce too many balls, you will want to incorporate many of the practical principles in the next chapter.

If you are one of those centered people who has a good sense about your life and purpose you may want to select a few of the upcoming principles in order to support and enhance what you are already doing.

Let's remember those rotting potatoes one more time! There is a stench that accompanies the rush toward uselessness on the part of those potatoes. Remember Lazarus! Our lives emit a sweet savor of life or the stench of death to those who are around us. Right now you are bringing one or the other savor to others.

Potatoes that have not fulfilled their purpose move toward the frenzied sprouting activity. People without purpose may exhibit the same kind of frenzy, burning themselves out as workaholics, supermoms or social animals.

When you have become clear about your life purpose, your roots are firmly planted. It is then you can bring life (sweet savor) to all who know you. The opposite is also true. If you are practicing hyperliving, skimming the surface of life, filling your days with activity, your words, actions, interests and attitude tend to bring the smell of death to all who know you.

What you give out is usually what you get back. This is a good reason to consider your frenzy level. If you are living congruently, your life may be full to the brim with activity, but this activity flows out of a sense of purpose. This purpose brings calm, which brings peace to others and you receive calm and peace in return.

Breathing Can Be the Beginning of Balance

One of the vital elements in being able to experience a Fresh Start is learning how to interrupt old habits, spring out of depression, regain your energy, put an end to frenzy and even find time to focus on a new beginning.

Breathing is available to every person in every situation. Mothers giving birth know the power of focusing on breathing patterns. Pain is reduced through increased oxygen to the muscles. Toxins are released, relaxation is enhanced. The chaotic mind is stilled.

Martial arts instructors teach the use of breathing for centering and generating power out of clarity of focus. Weight lifters utilize breath as a part of their physiological strength. Many others, including athletes, musicians and speakers would agree on the value of proper breathing techniques. Without understanding the more complex aspects of using the breathing process you can simply turn your attention to your breathing. This tends to focus you on the heavenly perspective of life.

For instance, when the feeling of being pressed for time overwhelms you, focus on breathing. As you drive to your appointment or return phone calls or think about what you have to do, breathe.

This is a baby step designed to bring you into a place to take a giant step. As you take this small step consistently you will be amazed at the miracles that will begin to unfold in your life.

An Additional Step

Share your commitment to breathing with two or three people who love you and are interested in their own personal growth. When you are together and a problem arises, remind one another to "Breathe!"

A Word to the Wise

This is it! This is your life. You are reading this book because you want to make some changes. So, be careful! Danger lurks in the shadow of wisdom revealed but unheeded. The practical expression of that solemn statement is this:

"Impression without expression leads to depression."

In other words, don't wait to act on the breathing exercise. Change is related to action as well as to knowledge. Those who loiter and languish, waiting for the happiness bus to pull up at their front door, will still be starving when the end comes. Your mind can become your worst enemy by offering thoughts like,

"This breathing thing is too simple."

"This sounds like some spiritual transcendental stuff. It's not for me."

"That might work, but I don't feel like doing it. It makes me feel silly or unnatural."

"I'll do it when I'm alone, or have some time, but not now."

Remember the graphic:

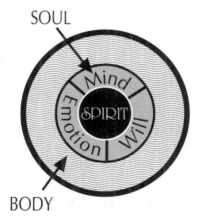

Your soul thrives on activity out of chaos. Your mind, as a major element in your soul, must be confronted by the real you. Access your spirit by breathing and centering on

your willingness to have a fresh perspective. This simple activity is a life-changing practical tool in the renewing of your mind. You will begin to live more consistently in your spirit because your transformed mind will quiet the chaos and remind you of your vision.

The Hidden Power in the Principle

I mentioned the potential for miracles inherent in the breathing exercise. The power hidden within the breathing goes beyond the physiological benefits. This power exceeds the soulish benefits of calming your mind and emotions.

As you breathe, the real you is being nurtured. Do you recall that God created Adam from the dust of the earth and "breathed into him the breath of life." You are developing the life-changing action of accessing the Breath of Life. Here, in your spirit, is where you will find your purpose, that unique calling for which you have been created.

CHAPTER 8

The Real You Now Becomes Visible

The potential for your Fresh Start is staggering when you realize that your unique destiny has been created in you. If we could actually put desires under a microscope like we now can with DNA, we could see the visions that are as uniquely yours as your DNA. The Creator has planted special longings in your heart.

While you were in the womb, your DNA building blocks were driving the design of your nose, brain, preferences, etc. (This doesn't exclude the role of environment.) You did not select your parents, your place in history, nor the geographical location of your birth. Neither could you control the tragedies or triumphs that may have come your way. (Perhaps your mother died when you were young, or your parents were famous, or financially you were able to study the violin, etc.) So you have some visible, measurable elements that have impacted and continue to impact your life. Less tangible but no less real are your inner dreams, desires and visions.

Utilizing Your Transformed Mind to Unlock the Invisible You

One of the best ways to tap into the real you is to get a fresh perspective, but other people can't see into your spirit. So I'm going to give you a unique way to access the wisdom written in your spirit. You will utilize your transformed mind to experience imaginary but potentially powerful insights into your inner self.

1. **Call in a Witness.**
    *   Imagine that you are looking at you through the eyes of someone who knows you very well and wants the best for you. What gifts and talents will you recognize as you look at yourself from a Witness perspective?

    _____

    _____

    *   What did you, as a Witness, see that pleased you the most?

    _____

    _____

2. **Call in a Creative Consultant.**
    *   Imagine that you have hired an intuitive, wise consultant who agrees with the Witness about your gifts and talents. What does this Consultant think you should do with some of your gifts and talents?

    _____

    _____

- Do you have any reasons or excuses why the Consultant's advice wouldn't work for you?

_____

_____

- Might your excuses be groundless if your circumstances were different?

_____

_____

3. **Call in a Dream Maker.**
   The Dream Maker is an imaginary person who has supernatural powers. He has only one restriction on working miracles: your desires must be heartfelt; no superficial requests allowed. Dream Maker wants to hear all your deepest desires. You may express as many of your heartfelt dreams, desires and goals as are important or exciting to you.
   What does your list look like?

_____

_____

_____

   Which two or three dreams stir your emotions most?

_____

_____

4. Call in a Career Consultant.

The Career Consultant will help you isolate your natural skills and talents and will need some answers to these questions:

- Think back to your first wage-earning job: What was it?

_____

_____

How did you feel about it?

_____

_____

List of some of the jobs you have had since then.

_____

_____

- Which two were your favorite? Why?

  ⇨ Favorite #1_____

  Why?_____

  ⇨ Favorite #2_____

  Why?_____

- What are the common denominators of the work you enjoyed most?

Examples:
- Worked outdoors
- Was my own boss
- Loved the team of people
- Great pay
- Liked the work itself because "I enjoy numbers, or research, or serving people, or the telephone, or selling"
- Enjoyed being the leader
- Received high recognition
- Utilized my creativity

Write a short paragraph about the common denominators in the work you liked.

_____

_____

_____

_____

Are you currently in a work environment that includes these common denominators?
Yes _____ No _____

Do you feel you need to make a major career change, minor alterations or no career change?
Major _____ Minor Alteration _____
No change. I love what I do! ___

Review the answers you have given your Career Consultant. What do you imagine the Consultant might suggest?

_____

_____

_____

5. Call in a Family Counselor

The Counselor is a sensitive, sensible psychologist who recognizes the importance of values in a family. You are seated comfortably and are sharing your own facts and feelings about those family members who are nearest and dearest to you.

- Who are the people you will mention as most important in your family circle?

_____

_____

- When you think of each one, what do you experience?

Example: Laughter, sense of sadness, not enough time together, closeness, sense of support, frustration, loneliness, isolation, intolerance, tension, strained relationships.

Your feelings may vary from person to person. Try to record specific feelings related to each person:

Family Member   Feeling

_____   _____

_____   _____

_____   _____

_____   _____

_____   _____

The Family Counselor is now going to provide some practical suggestions (baby steps) to enhance your family relationships. What will the Counselor suggest to you as action steps to be taken with specific members of your family?

_____

_____

_____

6. **Call in a Scribe!**
   Now you need an official secretary to whom you can dictate answers to very important questions. You will be taking this information to an important meeting so your Scribe must be accurate and efficient!
   ⇨ Recall your happiest childhood memories. What were your favorite things to do?

_____

_____

_____

   ⇨ When were you having the most fun?

_____

_____

⇨ What were your favorite games?

_____

_____

⇨ As a teenager or young adult what leisure activities
gave you the most enjoyment?

_____

_____

_____

⇨ Name at least 15 things you now enjoy. They may
even be work related. Just be sure to find a minimum of 15.

_____	_____	_____
_____	_____	_____
_____	_____	_____
_____	_____	_____
_____	_____	_____
_____	_____	_____

Now you need to brainstorm with your Scribe
about your answers. Review all the notes. Create a
summary statement, such as, "The activities that
have given me the most joy are_____
_____."

Examples: Outdoor fun, thinking activities, group
endeavors, solitary activities, (walking,
reading, computer games, writing, etc.),

musical experiences, family adventures/activities, sports (team sports or individual sports).

Your Summary Statement

_____

_____

_____

Can you incorporate more of these activities into your current life? Are some baby steps hidden in this list? What are they?

_____

_____

_____

7. **Call in Your Ideal Self.**
   There is an ideal part in you. Think of some people you admire in a special way. They may be people you have known, historical persons, alive, dead or even imaginary!

   Select three or four people whom you admire. These people have impacted your life personally—a parent, a teacher, an employer, etc. List their names and admirable qualities.

   Name   Qualities

   _____   _____

   _____   _____

   _____   _____

Are there any common denominators among them?
What are they?

Examples: Enthusiastic, optimistic, astute in business,
wise about life, sacrificial in service to others, humanitarian, highly spiritual, inven-
tive, creative, loving, kind, literary, musical,
athletic.

_____

_____

_____

By now you probably have had some Aha! experiences
about yourself. The Spirit at work in you will bring a sense
of direction and purpose to as you continue to consider
these insights. There is a transformational process at work
in you. This is the amazing Art of Your Fresh Start!

More exciting insights are coming!

CHAPTER 9

You Are Ready for a Summit Conference!

A benefit of a meeting like this is the anticipation of meaningful results. Usually summit meetings produce a positive new direction for the participants. Sometimes a treaty is signed, halting previous activities and instituting fresh directives or guidelines. Creativity springs out of a variety of viewpoints and ideas. The results can be revolutionary. The whole can be greater than the sum of the parts!

So, you are invited to attend a Summit Conference. The other attendees who have received official invitations are: The Witness, The Family Counselor, The Creative Consultant, The Scribe, The Dream Maker, Your Ideal Self, The Career Consultant.

You may want to invite, in your imagination, another participant: someone you especially trust, or who has been a help to you before, or whose opinion you value.

Who will you invite?

_____

_____

_____

Examples: The Spirit of God, your spouse, a special
friend, a business partner, your accoun-
tant, an attorney, a spiritual advisor.

The Subject of the Conference—
You and Your Life

This will be a life-changing conference! Decide where
and when it will be held. Here are some considerations for
your use in planning.

YOUR CONFERENCE PLANNING SHEET

DATE: _____
(Select a day when you will have time to focus.)
TIME:_____
(You may want to allow at least three hours.)
LOCATION: _____
(Since all the attendees are imaginary, you can choose
any location. It should be quiet and conducive to concen-
tration and creativity. Maybe an inspirational view or a fire-
place and hot coffee would be helpful.
ATTIRE:_____
I recommend your most-comfortable-to-dream-in
clothes.
MENU: _____
Sometimes physical food helps feed your spirit.

MATERIALS

You will need:
- ⇨ Your copy of *The Art of the Fresh Start*.
- ⇨ Two or three good pens and/or sharp pencils.
- ⇨ Any and all notes you have made prior to the conference.
- ⇨ A special notebook dedicated to you alone.
- ⇨ Any other books that are inspirational or thought provoking.
- ⇨ Any other supplies helpful for brainstorming, e.g., flip chart, markers, pillow, tape recorder, blank tapes, music.

Questions You Want Answered

Prior to the Summit, make a list of questions for which you want meaningful insights. Creating your list of questions will help you focus on the subject of the meeting, which is: *You and Your Life.*

Quest ons I Will Bring to the Summit Conference:

_____

_____

_____

_____

_____

_____

_____

_____

_____

_____

Summary

As you see, this is a creative way to access the unique you. You will begin to clarify your purpose as you focus on this Summit Conference experience.

It is important that you prepare to treat the next chapter as you would an actual retreat. If you do not have time to focus for two or three hours, I recommend that you skip the next chapter until you can use the Conference Planning Sheet and establish a time and place to concentrate.

The next chapter will be one of the most important turning points in your life. Approach it prayerfully and expectantly.

CHAPTER 10

Your Summit Experience!

You are about to embark on a fascinating experience. Let's review your readiness level.

Physical Preparation

1. Do you have all your supplies as listed on your Conference Planning Sheet in Chapter Nine?
2. Do you have a comfortable and distraction-free location?
3. Do you need to make any adjustments to give undivided attention to this experience? (Phone shut off? Comfortable place to write? etc.)

Spiritual Preparation

Are you expecting God's presence and love? By faith are you counting on His wisdom? Ask Him to open up His plans for you.

Mental Preparation

Remember the breathing exercise? It is the practical process for quieting your soulish mind and moving into your transformed mind.

- Breathe deeply
- Relax your muscles
- Exhale fully
- Inhale fully
- Be aware of listening

Let the Conference Begin!

There is a format arranged for this summit meeting. We will begin with roll call. Let's go around the circle and see who is here:

Let's review each of these participants.

The Witness—knows you very well.

The Creative Consultant—recognizes and understands the value of your gifts and talents.

The Dream Maker—has the miraculous ability to function in the world of the supernatural.

The Career Consultant—is educated, understands the world of work and the need to do satisfying work.

The Family Counselor—understands the importance of your most meaningful relationships.

The Scribe—conveys the facts you provided about your leisure life.

The Ideal You—knows what you value in ideal people.

The Special Guest—you invited, has a unique perspective.

Is everyone present? Can you see them and sense their wisdom and insight?

The Conference Format

There are four segments to this conference, which takes place with the participants gathered around a table. Participants place ideas or suggestions on the table. The real you uses the flip chart to identify the Aha! moments. You will ask your team for feedback.

Segment One
Question: What is Working in My Life?

Ask each participant to answer this question by placing some thoughts on the table. Unlimited ideas and observations can be given by each participant.

The Flipchart

Consider carefully all the wonderful observations participants make about you. Select the ones that you agree with wholeheartedly. Write them on the flipchart.

NOTE: You may want to review the notes you made in Chapter Eight.

What *Is* Working in My Life?

1. _____
2. _____
3. _____
4. _____
5. _____
6. _____
7. _____
8. _____

Segment Two
Question: What Shackles Do I Need to Shed?

Remember, these participants love you. They're not accusers. They feel that you are missing some joy and peace and direction in your life because of some soul-life fears or concerns. They will give you some answers to consider.

What Shackles Do I Need to Shed?

1. _____

2. _____

3. _____

4. _____

5. _____

6. _____

7. _____

8. _____

Segment Three
Question: What One Practical Suggestion Would You Give Me to Enhance My Life Experience?

Return now to Chapter Eight and review what insights each participant gave you earlier. What creative suggestions would be natural for each one to give you? This is a very important question.

Which of these creative considerations trigger your greatest sense of excitement or good feelings? Put a star by them on your flipchart.

What One Practical Suggestion Would You Give Me to Enhance My Life Experience?

1. _____
2. _____
3. _____
4. _____
5. _____
6. _____
7. _____
8. _____

Segment Four
Question: What Does the Ideal You Look Like?

Ask each participant to give responses that are most congruent with who you are as they know and love you.

Example: The ideal you will live in the country and own your own business.

What Does the "Ideal Me" Look Like to You?

1. _____
2. _____
3. _____
4. _____
5. _____
6. _____
7. _____
8. _____

Get Your Palette and Paint Brush

You have experienced some intuitive responses as you considered thoughtfully each of the four segments of your conference. Now let your creative self, the real you, paint a picture of your ideal future.

The Landscape of Your Life

Consider all the insights you have gained and create a physical representation of some of these. You may want to get a huge piece of paper and do some sketching. Or you may want to cut pictures from magazines and put them in a photo album as your dream book. Or you may choose bold, single words to represent your insights. Perhaps your sense of purpose will appear here.

The Closing Session of the Summit Conference

You have received a lot of input. Absorb the ideas that have given you joy or enthusiasm. More has happened at the conference than you might be aware of at this moment. Don't move into your chaotic mind and try to sort out this experience. Simply continue to watch, wait and listen.

Summary of Book One

The Landscape of Your Life exercise was the final activity for laying the foundation for your Fresh Start. Before moving to Book Two you may want to review what you have discovered. Perhaps you will choose to share your insights with a loved one. Be sure your VISION is clear. You are now going to discover The "How" of Maintaining Your Fresh Start.

BOOK TWO

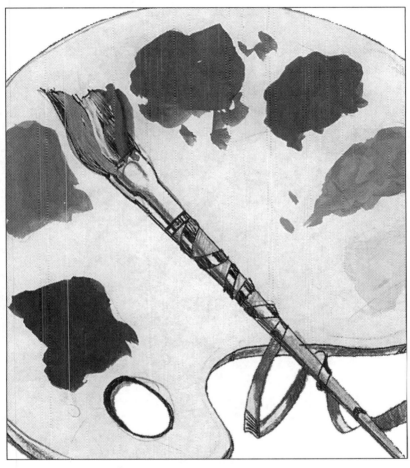

The "How" of
Maintaining Your
Fresh Start

Introduction

You have identified the frenetic activity factor and the emotional rollercoaster of soul-life, and now you see the real you more clearly. The challenge is to learn how to transfer out of the living death of frantic activity and maintain your sense of vision and purpose on a regular basis.

Not long ago I visited an unhappy middle manager of an East Coast company. Jan was recently divorced, had been passed over for a promotion, had gained weight and was even considering suicide. I responded to her recounting of her concerns with, "Jan, you need a Fresh Start. You need to see who you are."

Her eyes were blank, without light, her mind preoccupied with trauma and tragedy. "How can I jump start myself when I'm dead inside, with no energy and no hope?" she asked.

Her question is absolutely and utterly the critical question. The answer is two-pronged: practical action and revelation. Jan wasn't emotionally ready for revelation, but she definitely needed some practical help!

If you're in the same place as Jan, this next section of *The Art of the Fresh Start* is just right for you. It provides the practical and critical actions to jump start a Fresh Start again and again.

These actions are lifetime elements for sustaining Fresh Starts every day. They are surefire—guaranteed to lift you to another realm of living.

These critical actions will continue to transform you, not because you grit your teeth and strive, but because you'll be drawn to two or three that you feel certain will be effective.

Faltering Faith

Many people want to explain their predicament to anyone who will listen, but they don't want solutions. To solutions they respond:

"I've already tried that."

"I can't do that because I don't have any money."

"I don't have time to do that."

"Yes, but my husband (wife, mother, boss, friend) wouldn't understand if I . . ." and on and on.

These are people who aren't desperate or disgusted enough yet. They are, in a warped way, still enjoying their misery. Sometimes the soul-life provides a hiding place where some people prefer to stay. It's a cave to hide in, to moan and complain, and hold daily pity-parties. No amount of logic or persuasion will move soul-life addicts into the spirit-life. We have all been stuck in our soulishness. Remember, the life of the Fresh Start in the spirit comes by revelation. Transferring out is triggered from the inside-out. Then, faith is available which supplies the energy for practicing the critical actions.

Testing Your Faith

You can discern easily where you are right now. You can check your spirit by asking yourself these two simple questions:

On a scale of 1-10, how high is my desire to vault out of my present experience and live on a more meaningful, fulfilling level? _____

On a scale of 1-10, how high is my willingness to act by faith and enter actively into practical activities to produce transformation in me? _____

As you respond to these questions, remember that change occurs as a result of your willingness, not your will! ("The spirit is willing but the flesh is weak.") Change occurs as you envision your ideal future, knowing that you will move toward what you think about. ("As a man thinketh in his heart so is he.") When you rest in willingness and vision by faith, transformation will occur from the inside-out.

Now you are prepared to consider critical actions to sustain your Fresh Start. Each of the following chapters is devoted to a practical way to live to fuel your inner life. There is power beyond your highest expectations hidden in the activity outlined in each chapter.

In fact, you will enter into a dimension of living that will surpass your greatest expectations if you dare to pursue each one by faith.

These nine life-changing activities are:

1. *Singing*

2. *Tapping into Your Passion*

3. *Displaying Your Enthusiasm*

4. *Rekindling Your Sense of Wonder and Curiosity*

5. *Considering the Invisible*

6. *Enhancing Your Sense of Humor*

7. *Asking Questions and Listening to the Answers*

8. *Practicing the Art of Loving*

9. *Defining Your Purpose in Life*

CHAPTER 11

Sing!

This simple, essential step is revolutionary in its power. You may have the ability to carry a tune, or you can put in a tape or play your own accompaniment. Here's how it works:

1. *Select two or three of your favorite songs, preferably songs to which you know the words. If not, make up words or hum enthusiastically.*

2. *Find a place where you can sing as loud as you want. You may need to get in your car, go to the basement, the garage, your closet or the shower. I encourage you to do this for a minimum of 5 to 10 minutes a day every day for at least 21 days.*

Jan, the depressed middle manager, couldn't bring herself to sing. Feeling bad was more rewarding for her than feeling good. Feeling bad is her reality for now. Nevertheless there is power inherent in singing when you feel enabled to sing.

The reason singing is so important, the reason it works, is two-fold. One, singing engages and stimulates both sides of the brain and brings a sense of balance. Two, when you're singing, there's little room left for worrying or fretting or complaining.

My favorite author, the Apostle Paul, affirms the value of singing. When giving directions about how to grow in faith, Paul wrote, ". . . be filled with the Spirit; speaking to yourselves in psalms, and hymns and spiritual songs, singing and making melody in your heart to the Lord."[1]

Scientists have research that confirms the soothing, healing, restorative power of music.

So make a joyful noise!

---

1. Eph. 5:19, 20.

CHAPTER 12

Tap into Your Passion

Remember that these actions are designed to jump-start you out of an uncomfortable or dissatisfied state. The actions are critical because they create good feelings in you. As Gary and Pat Emery write, "Good feelings allow your true self to appear and lead to your real purpose."[1] The critical actions are practical steps for creating the good feelings that give you the power to experience a Fresh Start.

The Passion Question

In their book *The Second Force*, the Emerys provide their strong insight into the power inherent in good feelings. They write, "Good feelings come from the absence of thought about what you need to be happy."[2]

In discussing the world of good feelings the Emerys say, "Bring good feelings to what you do and you'll have no need

1. Gary Emery and Pat Emery, *The Second Force* (New York: NAL-Dutton 1990), 94.
2. Emery and Emery, 90.

for cookbook solutions. What you need to do next comes before you ask—you have intuitive flashes and hunches about what to do . . . Start with a good feeling and you naturally and spontaneously do what needs to be done."[3]

This next critical action of accessing your passion is critical because it puts you in touch with your unique good feelings. The brain does not know the difference between fact and fiction and it responds, chemically, to the images the mind focuses on. For instance, if you think you hear an intruder at your back door in the middle of the night, you may break into a cold sweat. That is a chemical reaction that produces a bad feeling.

Thus, it becomes crucial to stay in touch every day with those things about which you are passionate. They produce good feelings!

Passion Exercise

Take a moment to practice a simple exercise. Bring to mind a person, place or thing that gives you great joy or pleasure. It may be a special child or a friend, a past or future trip, your faith, a cherished dream, etc. Now, stand up, count to three, think of this person, place or thing and shout an enthusiastic "YES!"

Now, check your spirit! Can you feel the bubbling life, the renewed energy, a new vitality? This is an action that will sustain you day after day.

Ongoing Passion

Continue to give focused thought to the pictures, visions, people, ideas, relationships, activities that give you the greatest sense of euphoria. These are things that give

---

3. Emery and Emery, 82, 83.

you feelings of peace, freedom, joy, pleasure, satisfaction, hope and fulfillment.

For instance, you may enjoy fishing on a quiet lake or walking under the stars. You may be excited about a new business you would like to create. Perhaps a gentle awareness that God loves you and is at work in your life creates your sense of euphoria.

Whatever these elements are in your life, consciously take time now to list at least four of them below:

_____   _____

_____   _____

_____   _____

Each moment of each day, when you sense your own energy dissipating, or when your feelings turn negative, or when your stress turns into distress, cast your inner glance upon those elements in your life that produce good feelings.

Notice carefully what I have said. Cast your *inner focus* on these elements. Once again you will notice that this is an inside-out activity. You shift your gaze, your focus, from disturbance to euphoria.

You can encourage your good feelings with actual pictures of your favorite serene lake, or your mate, or a map of a place you're going to visit. And you can remove or avoid negative feelings by shutting off the television or refusing to read or listen to depressing news! What you're doing is creating an environment conducive to healthy personal growth, which is quite different from ignoring or denying reality. These baby steps can have powerful results and the good feelings that flow from your action will move you toward an even greater sense of purpose and direction.

Your feel-good state will cause you to touch the lives of others in a positive, powerful manner. They, in turn, will respond by feeling good themselves and their responses enhance you and others further.

Can you sense the potential in this critical action as you practice it continuously in every situation in your life?

CHAPTER 13

Display Your Enthusiasm

Displaying your enthusiasm feeds your own spirit!

Jim and I were traveling in Kenya a few years ago. We hired a driver and began a tour of the bush in a Land Rover. As I watched our route on the map I realized the next village was situated right on the equator. I thought it would be fun to experience standing on the equator. We climbed out of our vehicle to survey the scenery. I always half-expected a line to be painted there on the ground as there is on our globe!

Suddenly I looked up to see a six-foot five-inch Masai warrior running toward us. He appeared to be about 25 years old, had a huge smile, and beautiful white teeth that would have made any orthodontist beam.

"I'm so glad you're here!" Sammy exclaimed breathlessly, causing me to wonder if we had an appointment. "Let me show you something!" He ducked behind a nearby tree and reappeared with an old aluminum bucket, a pink plastic pitcher full of water, a funnel and a straw basket of loose grass clippings. "Watch this!"

He poured the water through the funnel, sprinkled the grass clippings on top to demonstrate the direction the water flowed. The water went straight through the funnel to the bottom of the bucket. He grinned broadly. "See there? That's because you're standing right on the equator! Watch this!"

Then he carried his equipment about 10 feet north of the invisible equator line. This time as he poured the water through the funnel and added the grass clippings, we watched the water swirl in a clockwise direction.

"Isn't that amazing?" he asked, obviously bemused by the phenomenon. He turned and walked 10 feet south of the imaginary line and repeated his demonstration. This time the water swirled counter-clockwise! "Isn't that incredible?" he grinned. We agreed and paid the handsome young entrepreneur for his efforts. Isn't that incredible?

How many times do you suppose he had given that little demonstration? Probably hundreds of times. But it was the first time for us, and Sammy captured us with his genuine enthusiasm. He had seen this entire demonstration through our eyes, watched our enthusiasm build and he himself was rejuvenated.

My Father's Enthusiasm

My father spent most of his career as a life insurance agent in central Illinois. He was a born salesman. He could visit with farmers, bankers, insurance company presidents and the local postmaster with equal ease and aplomb.

Also, he was a born philosopher. Our family lived on top of a hill that overlooked the Illinois River Valley. As a young adult my favorite moments were spent in a lawn chair perched in the grass, sipping a freshly brewed mug of coffee, musing about life with this congenial patriarch. He had insights about the big picture that continue to influence my life.

One Saturday night, under a full moon, with crickets chirping and fireflies twinkling, I asked my dad what his purpose in life was. I was having some philosophical struggles of my own about then. He laughed gently at my seriousness, but his response was heartfelt. "My goal is simple. Each day I want to make people glad they saw me."

That was it, plain and simple. His focus wasn't selling insurance policies, it was lighting up peoples' lives. He even had a standing offer to any Illinois State Police officer. "If you recognize my license plate and stop me, I will buy you a cup of coffee and a steak dinner, anytime, day or night."

In those casual coffee stops my dad wrote life insurance policies. But, above all, he made and kept lifetime friends. My philosopher father fulfilled his purpose every day of his life. His purpose for being was far bigger than making a sale, or paying the mortgage or buying groceries.

And, because Dad's purpose was also his passion, he enjoyed virtually every day of his life. Even in some desperate circumstances, his laughter and care for people reigned. Through his own personal challenges as a young husband and father, he had learned to value the privilege of having been called to make a positive contribution to the life experience of others.

When he was 74 years old, my dad had a massive stroke. Though his mind remained strong and astute, he could no longer walk or talk. During the last five years of his life after the stroke, Dad was in and out of hospitals for therapy. When he would leave, nurses and therapists would weep. He could give motivational speeches with the smile on his face, the light in his eyes, one syllable of speech and the lilt in his voice. He was still fulfilling his purpose the Sunday morning he died in Los Alamitos Hospital in Southern California.

In observing this man live his life, I saw the power of personal enthusiasm displayed toward others. In the 49 years I knew him, never once do I recall my father complaining about problems or negative circumstances. He had his trials and tribulations, but he remained faithful to his purpose to "make other people glad they saw me." As a result, his own spirits stayed high.

Some critics might say, "That seems phony to me. Why should I pretend to be happy or enthusiastic when I'm not?" There are several solid answers to this logic, but first, let's look at the spirit behind the question. Is this the attitude of one who aspires to be happy, or is this one of those people who prefers being miserable? If "phoniness" popped into your mind, you might want to test your own preference.

The truth about enthusiasm is closely related to those good feelings we discussed in the previous chapter. What you sow is what you reap. When you sow enthusiasm and good feelings in the lives of others, you experience abundance. If you access your passions regularly, you will display the authentic enthusiasm that springs from this river of life within you.

Dr. Albert Mehrabian, a behavioral scientist from the University of California in Los Angeles, underscores the power of displayed enthusiasm in his research on people's responses to one another. In his paper *Silent Messages* he reports that 55 percent of our effect on others is body movement, 38 percent is tone of voice—the key factor being the presence or absence of a smile—and the remaining 7 percent is based on your knowledge.

The application of Dr. Mehrabian's research is simple and life-changing. You and I create the ongoing energy to live a sustained life of purpose and meaning by daring to demonstrate our love and enthusiasm to others! Our walk and talk is more important than knowledge. A display of caring renews the giver as well as the receiver.

Practice Smiling by Faith!

The result will be the returned smiles of others, which triggers the good feelings, which results most often with you remaining in your spirit.

CHAPTER 14

Rekindle Your Sense of Wonder and Curiosity

The visible, tangible, material world consumes most of our time, energy and attention. Consider, for instance, your normal daily routine—showering, teeth brushing, making coffee, driving in the traffic, handling paperwork, attending meetings, making phone calls, grocery shopping, cooking, eating, laundry—most of the endless activity is devoted to sustaining the body. You may use your mind, but the reason for using it is to perform tasks, to generate a wage, to create creature comfort.

The consequence of this routine can be cynicism, boredom and burnout. The focus on the same old patterns at work and the ongoing chores at home can cause loss of perspective, a sense of purposelessness.

I recall visiting with a middle-aged man who sat next to me on a business trip. "Tell me what you do," I said.

"I'm a male nurse in the psychotic ward at the University of California in Irvine."

Fascinated, I asked, "Do you like your job?"

"Oh yes, I love my job!"

"Really!" I said, encouraged by his enthusiasm. "Tell me what it is you like about your job."

"In my job the customer is always wrong!" he said, deadpan.

I laughed, but then I realized that this once compassionate nurse had become cynical about patients and caregiving. He needed a Fresh Start desperately. Making a New Year's resolution to care more for others or to enjoy work more wouldn't be enough to renew his spirit.

Often renewal comes when you transfer from the visible world to the invisible world. The trigger point of transferring may come when the mind can no longer comprehend the magnitude of a wonder-producing experience; it has to expand beyond normal boundaries to take in infinity.

A few months ago my husband and I were in Kaanapali, Maui. We went to the roof of the Hyatt Hotel to experience the planetary program given there. It was a gorgeous August night and the Persiades star showers were active.

The powerful telescope transplanted me emotionally out into the solar system! The craters on the moon were so vivid they seemed touchable. There were clusters of what the guide called "newborn stars." As we watched the occasional falling star it was staggering to realize that the star actually fell millions of years ago and the light was only now getting within range of our vision.

Moments like these—in nature, or with animals (like our gorilla experience) or listening to beautiful music—are essential to restoring a larger perspective to our comprehension of life, living, and purpose. What experiences are most uplifting for you? When do you experience the most inner restoration?

_____

_____

_____

_____

In addition, what are some activities that might generate those feelings but that you haven't experienced yet?

Examples:
> *A visit to the Grand Canyon*
> *Piloting an airplane*
> *A hunting trip to Montana*
> *A trip to the Louvre*
> *A morning spent in a worship service*
> *Opening night at the Vienna Opera*
> *A visit to the local animal shelter*
> *Rereading the heartwarming stories in* Chicken
> Soup for the Soul[1]
> *Watching an animal give birth*
> *Hiking on the John Muir trail*
> *A visit to the California Redwoods*
> *Sitting on the beach in Hawaii*

Create your own list of experiences you would like to have:

_____

_____

_____

---

1. Jack Canfield and Mark Victor Hansen, *Chicken Soup for the Soul* (Deerfield Beach, Florida: Health Communications, Inc., 1993).

_____

_____

You will rekindle your sense of wonder by consciously building these experiences into your life. Failure to do so can cause discontent and even discouragement.

A Heart Resolution

If you sense your own inner yearning for a restored enthusiasm for life, what might you select as your activity for this month?

_____

_____

_____

Do you have a desire to incorporate some of these experiences into your life on a regular basis? You may want to look at your calendar and create a place for these activities. This becomes a key ingredient in designing your life experience based on the desires planted in your heart. That distinguishes a heart resolution from a contrived scheme or goal. Your consistent results will be amazing.

The Pharaoh Quail Story

There is another huge benefit for designing those wonder-producing experiences into your life. Your capacity to expect and experience miracles will expand immeasurably!

My personal experience continues to show me that my faith increases as I walk in the realm of wonder and expectation. God seems to take great delight in demonstrating both His presence and His sovereignty through the serendipities and so-called coincidences in our lives.

One of the most dramatic experiences in my life was divinely designed to restore and renew my sense of wonder. I was teaching a night class, called "The Bible As Literature," in adult education at California State University in Bakersfield, California.

One Monday evening the topic was miracles and the subject matter focused on the Israelites in the wilderness. I explained that the Hebrews were tired of manna and were murmuring about their longing for fresh meat. Suddenly quail began to fall from the sky according to the Old Testament account. I cited the research of Werner Keller in *The Bible As History*. Keller explained that the quail in the Red Sea region migrate in the spring. The seasonal winds are very strong in this area. The birds become winded and fall to the ground. This was God's means of supply for the Israelites, according to Mr. Keller.[2]

Without warning an older man in the back row of the class jumped to his feet and shouted, "Lady, that's the dumbest thing I've ever heard. You must not be a hunter. Quail are ground birds. They don't migrate 2,000 miles at a time."

While I was scrambling to keep my composure a man in the front row stood and responded. "Excuse me," he said, "I'm the only pharaoh quail raiser in the United States, and the pharaoh quail, also known as the Egyptian quail, is the only quail that migrates 2,000 miles at a time." There he was! The only Egyptian quail raiser in the country in my class when I needed him!

Logical explanations fail in the face of "pharaoh quail" experiences. We've all had implausible events that caused

2. Werner Keller, *The Bible As History* (New York: William Morrow and Co., 1964), 115, 131.

us to wonder, to be curious, to sense the world of the transcendent, but most of us stop there. If our minds haven't been transformed by the experience, we will rush back to the familiar issues of routine existence.

Enhancing Your Wonder in the Midst of the Mundane

"Pharaoh quail" experiences aren't ordinary. Some days you need to take baby steps to help cultivate your sense of wonder.

Activity #1
Approach Each Day as a Student of People, Service and Quality.

My oldest daughter has confirmed the power of this. Monica keeps four daily journals going all the time. She began this habit as a teenager. In our philosophical discussions as a mother and daughter she asked me questions. If she deemed my response insightful or wise, she recorded it in her journal. Over the years this practice has resulted in her being a keen observer of life.

Today Monica is married with two small children. Her diaries include observations on the gifts, talents and uniqueness of each of her boys. In addition she maintains a "Miracle Diary" in which she records prayer requests and answers. Over the years Monica has seen some amazing answers to prayer. If she wants to rekindle her sense of wonder, she need only review her notes!

You may choose to create your own personal Aha! journal. This is not necessarily a daily diary, but more of a reflective activity during times of high stress, unsettling circumstances or change.

Recording your own insights, thoughts and lessons learned helps keep you attuned to a larger perspective of life. You will experience moving out of your body pre-occupation (visible issues) and bypassing your mental pre-disposition to worrying (soul-life). The real you becomes present (spirit-life) as you respond reflectively rather than in the knee-jerk mode.

Professionally you may find your circumstances creating unhappiness, irritation or frustration in your life. As you see this happening, dare to focus on all the solution options. Become a student of your circumstances. Create a journal of professional insights. Record your concerns in one column and potential solutions in another. For example:

Concerns	**Possible Solutions**
1. My assistant comes in late two days a week and the rest of the team has to do her work. They resent her and so do I. The phones aren't being covered and even clients are upset.	1. Issue a written warning.
	2. Find out why she is late and help her solve her problem.
	3. Put her on probation.
	4. Fire her.
	5. Move her to another department.
	6. Take her to lunch and communicate her options to her.
	7. Relocate myself in the company.

This activity begins to trigger your curiosity and your anger ebbs away as your mind is preoccupied with finding solutions. This same approach can be applied to concerns in relationships, parenting and difficult decisions.

Activity #2
Ask Your Braintrust!

You have some special people in your life who love you unconditionally and whose wisdom you value and trust. Seek these individuals out and describe briefly a concern you may have. Ask them to give you four or five creative insights into the problem or five suggestions for solutions.

Your role is to listen, take notes and receive the input. Do not explain to them why their insights are wrong or why their suggestions won't work.

You are developing your curiosity as you observe a situation from the viewpoint of someone else.

Activity #3
Actively Seek Out Great Music and Art.

Great music and great art inspire a sense of wonder, especially the old masters. When was the last time you actively sought out the symphony? How recently have you gone alone to a fine museum and stood quietly in front of the inspiring works of Rembrandt or Michelangelo?

These simple steps rekindle the real you. Hidden in your spirit are gifts and talents you have yet to discover. Possibilities will stir within you.

Activity #4
Delve into Something Totally Different.

Not long ago I became aware of my fascination with log homes, large fireplaces and the country look. However, Scottsdale, Arizona, is not exactly log-cabin country so I went to a bookstore and selected *Log Home Living* magazine for an evening of relaxing and renewal. Now I subscribe to the magazine. Each month when my copy arrives I wonder what it would be like to build a log home in the desert.

After our experience of viewing the stars and moon on the roof of the Maui Hyatt, I bought *Sky and Telescope Magazine.* Reading about topics that are foreign to us reminds us how much there is to know and how many places there are to go. These activities will lift us out of our ruts and routines.

Activity #5
Examine Your Routines and Consciously Make Small Changes.

Recently I asked a seminar audience to shout out some routine activities that have become boring habits. One of the men responded, "Kissing my wife good-bye each morning." After his colleagues had a good-humored, empathetic laugh, I suggested he stop, gather her up passionately and kiss her as if it was the last time ever he might express his love for her!

He grinned and said, "If I try that I'll be late for work!"

After the laughter subsided we brainstormed several routine functions that could be changed to rekindle a sense of awareness and stimulate a sense of wonder. Some of these included:

- Change the route you take to work.
- Shop in a different supermarket.
- Take a bath instead of a shower.
- Shut off the TV.
- Put new pictures on your desk.
- Rearrange the furniture.

Time-Out

Take a few moments and list as many ideas as possible that would represent even a slight change from your current routines.

Tap Other Sources for Fresh Ideas

The world famous interior designer Alexandra Stoddard offers hundreds of suggestions and creative ideas for turning your "dull, irritating routines into life-enhancing rituals." Her book *Living the Beautiful Life* will inspire you to get beyond your routine life experience.[3] For instance, she suggests "dressing for dinner at home" as a change of routine.

Jim and I decided to incorporate her idea to change our New Year's Eve routine into a ritual. We turned down invitations to the typical parties and for the last three years have created our own private New Year's Eve celebration. Jim dresses in his tuxedo, I put on a long gown. We light the candles, barbecue a filet and share intimate elegance. Then we play our favorite CDs and dance for an hour or two. This is a great way for us to have a Fresh Start in our relationship for the new year.

Other ideas from Alexandra's book include:

- Make lobster, avocado and wild rice salad for a picnic.
- In autumn go to see the fall foliage and pick apples.
- Give each dinner guest a tiny present.
- Make Sunday night special. Create a ritual that punctuates the end of one week and the beginning of the next.

---

3. Alexandra Stoddard, *Living the Beautiful Life* (New York: Avon Books, 1986), 84-86.

CHAPTER 15

Consider the Invisible

It's important to recognize that the miraculous is not necessarily tied to the religious realm. The miraculous realm usually is in the invisible dimension, which is the dimension man was created to live in and from which we have been virtually disconnected through our preoccupation with body and soul. The religious realm, on the other hand, is about outward form and rituals.

Frank Tipler, a well-known mathematical physicist, has utilized the laws of physics and mathematics to examine the measurable possibility of proving, not only that God exists, but that all life is destined for resurrection. Tipler presents his conclusions in his book *The Physics of Immortality*. As a professed atheist he made an amazing turnabout as a result of the data.[1]

---

1. As reported in *Personal Update, Newsletter of Koinonia House*, Volume 5, No. 1 (January 1995): 9. [Frank Tipler, *The Physics of Immortality* (New York: Doubleday, 1994.)]

Many times we need to simply open ourselves to fresh ideas, to be curious. This sense of curiosity can be the trigger that opens revolutionary insight for you as it apparently did for Frank Tipler.

Software, Hardware and the Information Age

As the world of technology expands at a mind-boggling pace, an interesting analogy becomes evident, one that enhances our awareness of the invisible.

Computer hardware is, of course, totally useless without software. In the same sense, the body is our "visible" hardware. The invisible information or software is analogous to the spirit. We can only see or experience information through the computer screen of the soul. All three components are essential and interactive. If the spirit is absent, so is the soul, and the screen is empty.

Modern physics proves that time is a physical property affected by mass, acceleration and gravity. The real you is software and has no mass. Therefore, you have no time dimension!

There is an interesting aside to these technological developments and insights. Many futurists, like John Naisbett, have predicted that the next century will be focused on the invisible world. Two of the "overarching trends influencing our lives" as we approach the 21st century, says Naisbett, are:

- A Renaissance in the Arts
- The Religious Revival of the New Millennium

Naisbett observes that "when people are buffeted about by change, the need for spiritual belief intensifies . . . Science and technology do not tell us what life means.

We learn that through literature, the arts, and spirituality."[2]

A Persian futurist who lived in the fifth century B.C. looked into the world of today and made some amazing observations. Daniel the prophet, an important leader in the country now called Iran, described our modern era: "Many shall run to and fro, and knowledge shall be increased."[3]

In other words, our knowledge increased dramatically (soul), and we are running "to and fro" in frenetic activity (body), but the results are painfully evident in a society of broken homes, abuse, drugs and dissatisfaction. About this Daniel said, "the wicked shall do wickedly; and none of the wicked shall understand; but the wise shall understand."[4]

Wisdom goes beyond information. It is an understanding that springs from the spirit. Technology can't supply the "heart" needed in our daily experience.

The Role of Intuition

Most of us have an idea what intuition means, but agreement on a firm definition isn't easy.

Webster's *New Twentieth Century Dictionary* defines intuition as:

1. *the immediate knowing or learning of something without the conscious use of reasoning; instantaneous apprehension*

2. *something known or learned in this way*

---

2. John Naisbett and Patricia Aburdene, Megatrends 2000 (New York: William Morrow & Co., Inc., 1990), 272.

3. Dan. 12:4.

4. Dan. 12:10.

Nancy Rosanoff in her book *The Intuition Workout* writes, "Intuition is when we know, but we don't know how we know." She says that individuals experience intuition in a variety of unique ways. She is a strong advocate of the need for people to utilize this additional way of knowing.[5]

Today's competitive environment tempts us to make decisions by looking at the outward circumstances instead of looking within and listening to the still small voice.

Edward McCracken, CEO of Silicon Graphics, a fast-growing computer company with $1.5 billion of annual sales, recognizes the crucial importance of intuition.

"The most important trait of a good leader is knowing who you are. In our industry very often we don't have time to think. You have to do all your homework, but then you have to go with your intuition without letting your mind get in the way."[6]

Joel Barker, well known in the business world for his use of the paradigm and paradigm-shift concepts, recognizes the critical role intuition will play in the 21st century. In his video, "Paradigm Pioneer," Barker suggests that one of the three vital elements for meaningful leadership in the future will be intuitive skills. Technology produces so much information that at some key juncture decisions must be made without all the facts, because the facts change by the second.

Wolf Schmitt, the CEO of Rubbermaid, credits intuition as a key factor in Rubbermaid qualifying as the most admired company in America. He says that the company's success revolves around a variety of maverick approaches to business. One approach is to overwhelm competitors by

---

5. Nancy Rosanoff, *The Intuition Workout* (New York: Aslan Publishing, 1991), 16.
6. Stratford Sherman, "Leaders Learn to Heed the Voice Within," *Fortune*, 22 Aug. 1994: 93.

flooding the market with new products. But the challenge lies in how to do that. "The first thing is to generate a huge quantity of ideas. We consider maybe 2,000 to 4,000 a year. Next is not to fool around, but intuitively—and very quickly—reduce that big number to one that makes sense." Schmitt encourages his managers to "go with the gut."[7]

Another Perspective on Intuition

Much of the recent research on male/female brain differences includes a discussion of human intuitive capacity and variation.

Through a sophisticated form of magnetic resonance imaging (MRI) on living brains, researchers have new data that may explain women's intuition.

A research team from Yale University School of Medicine gave language tasks to 19 men and 19 women. The researchers then watched their brain activity using the MRI. Men activated an area on the left side of the brain while women engaged the left side and a comparable area on the right side.[8]

Genetics expert Anne Moir reports similar research results in her book, *Brain Sex*. Through work on brain autopsies it is clear that the corpus callosum—the mass of fibers connecting the brain's right and left hemispheres—is larger in proportion to brain weight in women than in men. Moir says more information is being exchanged between the two hemispheres in women. Moir feels this could account for women sensing intuitively what is happening around them because they process the facts emotionally as well as mentally.

---

7. Thomas J. Martin, "How to Grow a New Product Every Day," *Fortune*, 14 Nov. 1994: 270.
8. Karen S. Peterson, "Battle of the Sexes Starts in the Brain", *USA Today*, 14 March 1995: 1D-2D.

In the midst of these sometimes controversial view-points about intuition, I would like to add the Fresh Start perspective. Consider this: Intuition involves the human spirit, plain and simple. This human spirit has the capacity to function well beyond the borders of soul or body. However, even the human spirit has limitations. To go beyond intuition is to experience the Spirit of God awakening your human spirit to the realm of His reality.

One step toward an awareness of the miraculous is to see that there is an invisible, intuitive dimension that is available to you. Your ability to access your intuitive side, using the critical actions we have been discussing, is key to living the inside-out life. This awareness allows you to transfer out of your mental whirl more often. You will find yourself moving toward the realm of faith and revelation. Continue to consider the invisible world.

Recognize the Miraculous

The critical action of considering the miraculous includes looking for and treasuring the manifestations of God's miraculous work in the concrete circumstances of life.

As you recall and recount the miraculous elements of life to others you will be transformed personally. And, you are actively delivering the invisible gifts of love, joy, peace, patience and kindness to others. In addition, you are delivering a foundation for hope.

A True Story

Thom and Lisa Hunter from Guthrie, Oklahoma experienced this miraculous realm through a bizarre set of circumstances. In his book, *Those Not-So-Still Small Voices*, Thom Hunter explains their experience as struggling young parents with five children. They were putting out a small weekly newspaper. After one particularly exhausting late night, Thom rose early and headed for the printer in Oklahoma City. Lisa stayed home to get the kids off to school and to call local utility companies begging for one more day of mercy because their payments were late.

Enroute to Oklahoma City, Thom pulled off the interstate into a rest stop after consuming a large soft drink for breakfast. As he passed the public pay telephone, it began to ring. No one was around and out of a habitual response to a ringing phone, Thom absent-mindedly picked up the phone.

"Hello?" he said. There was dead silence and then a loud scream.

"Thom! What on earth are you doing at the electric company?" It was Lisa's voice at the other end.

"Lisa? What on earth are you doing calling the pay phone at a rest stop?"

The number of the electric company and the pay telephone differed by only one digit. But Thom and Lisa knew this was far beyond the world of probability. The two exclaimed and marveled and then they began the first authentic, uninterrupted, heart-to-heart conversation they had known in months.

As Thom writes, ". . . we could only suppose God knew we both needed, more than anything else that morning, each other's voices. He connected us."[9]

Thom and Lisa made some definite changes in their life. They realized they had become so devoted to building a career they had lost touch with building a life.

---

9. Thom Hunter, "Getting Connected," *Reader's Digest*, January 1995: 175, 176. [Thom Hunter, *Those Not-So-Still Small Voices* (Colorado Springs: NavPress, 1993).]

NOTE: Thom thinks God must have a sense of humor because two years later he had a new job, with the telephone company.

Consider the Ingredients in Their Story

The disastrous recipe for an outside-in life was in place:

- Preoccupation with work
- No quality time together
- Working to the exhausted state
- No meaningful communication
- Preoccupation with meeting body issues
- Functioning with the mental stress of worries and mental concerns

They needed a Fresh Start! Do you remember our discussion about the need to be disgusted with your life before you are ready for the Fresh Start? Sometimes transformational turning points occur in the midst of utter exhaustion and emptiness! Divine intervention (revelation) is at work.

A Ray of Hope

If you are feeling hopeless or weary or without the strength to get your life together, start celebrating! Those feelings are often the darkness before the dawn. Your body and soul approach have not created the quality of life you want. Now the real you is about to break forth!

A Turning-Point Experience

Thom and Lisa Hunter experienced God virtually calling them on the telephone in order to transfer them into the realm of True Reality. They became aware of an entirely different lifestyle, a quality of life that flows from the inside-out.

When the invisible world of the miraculous breaks into your life, there are usually some common elements:

- A turning-point experience, sometimes referred to as a wake-up call

- An emotional shift that includes a new dimension of spiritual understanding

- A new appreciation of what really matters in life

Have you had turning points in your life? Where were you? What were you doing? What were the euphoric feelings you experienced? Are you looking for evidence of God's hand in your life?

Sometimes you may get only a gentle nudge, a sunset, a rainbow, a new baby. Sometimes the invisible seeks us in health problems, tragedy and disappointment.

A Tragic Nudge

A few years ago I was preparing to speak to the front-line team of a group of electric utility company employees. Just two hours before my presentation, one of the seminar participants came to tell me of a tragic accident that had occurred the day before.

Linda, one of the line crew, had fallen from a platform where she was working and was killed instantly by the impact. One of her best friends gathered her belongings from her locker. Apparently Linda had shared dinner at her parents' home the night before her death. Her mother had packed a lunch for her from the leftovers. She had also written a love note and slipped it into Linda's lunch pail. Her friend found the note in the uneaten lunch:

Dearest Linda,

It's always great to have you here and also to have you eat your supper with us. I like to cook for more than two people, so please come often.

I'm happy I have a special daughter and a best friend—YOU! I think about you working in the cold and getting so many hurt toes and fingers. Please be careful because I love you very much.

Mom

Just knowing about Linda's story tends to move me into the realm of my spirit. No one needs to draw me a picture about the invisible realm, and I have a heightened desire to live in that awareness every day of my life. What about you?

A Corporate Nudge

Fortune magazine recounts the story of Willow Shire, a former vice-president at Digital Equipment Corporation, responsible for $900 million in annual sales to the healthcare industry.

Shire recounts that her marriage came apart as a result of inattention while she worked long hours with virtually no days off. Within months Digital's sales and marketing chief eliminated her job as well. She came face-to-face with an "unexamined life."

"Like countless people walloped by workplace change, Shire is searching for ways to change herself. Executives generally aren't an introspective lot, but in the dawn of the New Economy—with no job security or clear career path, with more responsibility and less certainty than ever— stressed-out managers increasingly are turning inside for answers," the article concludes.[10]

---

10. Sherman, 92, 93.

Your Personal Nudge

What messages have you received recently that might be God's wake-up call in your life? Many times we receive gentle nudges that are not easily recognizable. Quietly consider your recent circumstances, thoughts, feelings or experiences.

Write down your feelings or insights about being nudged.

_____

_____

_____

_____

_____

_____

_____

Remember, the inside-out life is the unique element in any Fresh Start. What are you doing to feed your spirit day by day?

_____

_____

_____

_____

CHAPTER 16

Enhance Your Sense of Humor

You might wonder what the connection is between increasing your laughter and creating a Fresh Start in your life. Perhaps you will be surprised to discover the powerful dimension humor brings to beginning again.

The Big Picture

Do you recall my friend Rosita Perez's story about little stuff and big stuff? Birth and death are big stuff, all the rest is little stuff. This sort of puts life into perspective, doesn't it?

That's what humor provides—perspective. Increasingly laughter is recognized as a powerful healing tool. That sage of long ago, King Solomon, said it best: "A merry heart doeth good like a medicine."[1] Maybe even better than

---

1. Prov. 17:22.

medicine, considering all the potential for negative side effects from trying to heal from the outside-in!

Belly laughter creates its own physiological/natural chemical power in the body which affects the mind, of course. Those now-famous endorphins seem to have all kinds of positive effects, don't they? The physical exercise that our internal organs get in belly laughter is a part of this amazing process. The body truly is "fearfully and wonderfully made."

Some of us see humor more easily than others. If you are not one who laughs uproariously, there are still some practical ways you can move toward the humorous perspective. As you sense your inner desire to lighten up, you will begin increasingly to have the inside-out view of the world. Little stuff dissipates more quickly! You are able to see more clearly what your purpose in life is when the little annoying distractions are not filling your field of vision.

Laughter in the Workplace

In a world filled with reengineering, downsizing and rightsizing, most companies are looking for ingenious ways to motivate their people and increase productivity, including incentive programs and quality circles. They are trying to do more with less.

However, employees claim that the factors that produce the best work environment come from another realm completely.

San Francisco business writers, Robert Levering and Milton Moskowitz, researched 147 work sites in the United States, asking employees what makes a company a great place to work. Their book, *The 100 Best Companies to Work for in America*, gives the results. The primary factors are "where you have laughter often, where the CEO knows everyone's name, and where workers feel like part of a team."[2] Happy workers provide better customer service, make fewer mistakes and will even trade off dollars in order to be in that kind of environment.

Stress results in major safety issues. Accidents and mistakes occur more often when employees are preoccupied with wondering when, and over what, the boss is going to have the next blow-up, or when they rush through a never-ending stream of responsibilities. Work that flows from the spirit rarely is tainted by the effects of preoccupation.

If you are a leader of people, you may want to reconsider your resolutions about improving time management, designing your five-year plan, and implementing a new sales incentive program. Perhaps your Fresh Start can begin from a revolutionary approach of really caring about and knowing your people, and letting them see your funny side.

Some practical ways to access your own spirit through humor:

1. Intentionally view a great movie once a week with your family. Suggestion: Take your children to the video store with you. They know what's funny.
2. Read the stories and jokes in *Reader's Digest* and other publications. Copy the items that strike you as genuinely funny. Retell them regularly and pass the copy around the office.
3. Do the same with cartoons that strike you as funny.
4. Keep a special Humor File in your desk. When you feel frustrated or explosive go through the file!

Some practical ways to create an environment of humor at the office:

---

2. *USA Today*, 25 Jan. 1993: 1A.

1. Appoint a Laughter Captain each month to look for creative ideas to bring humor into the work environment.
2. Create a Laff Box for humorous ideas, articles or stories. The Laughter Captain shares them with the group.
3. Declare a Crazy Hat Day at work.
4. Pass around a rotating Dunce Hat worn by a person who made the most recent dumb mistake.
5. Build humor into meetings through silly or interesting activities. For instance, tape a $5 bill under one chair; have an office treasure hunt.
6. Give an annual Humor Award that is worth real dollars. The winner is selected by co-worker votes based on having contributed the most to the positive atmosphere.
7. Read some good books on humor.

Remember, the reason for this focus is to clear out the soul-life, revitalize the body and get back in touch with the spirit. The ultimate result will affect the company's bottom line positively.

I have suggested that you keep a file on some of the things that strike your funnybone. One of my favorite stories appears in my good friend Naomi Rhode's book More Beautiful Than Diamonds.[3]

> *The cruise ship reached warm Jamaican waters and it was the night when dinner meant formal dress. At one end of the table, a man noticed the woman next to him was wearing a diamond pendant. It was just about the biggest diamond he had ever seen.*

---

3. Naomi Rhode, More Beautiful Than Diamonds (Nashville: Thomas Nelson Publishers, 1991), 102.

"I hope you don't mind my saying so, but that diamond is beautiful," he said.

She smiled pleasantly.

"I don't mind at all, and thank you," she said. "It's the Klopman diamond."

The guy looked puzzled.

"I've heard of the Hope diamond and some others," he said, "but the Klopman is a new one to me."

The woman explained the Klopman diamond was much like the Hope diamond, though somewhat smaller. However, the cut was identical and it was equal in quality. The Klopman even came with a curse, the same as the Hope diamond.

"That's astonishing, and it comes with a curse?" the man asked.

The woman nodded.

"If you'll forgive my curiosity, what kind of a curse?" he asked.

"Mr. Klopman."

> ALEX THIEN
> Milwaukee Sentinel

Part of the humor in this story rests in the reality of tradeoffs. Nothing in life is perfect, so why not approach the not-so-perfect with a sense of humor?

Your Funny Bone

What steps could you take to enhance your ability to laugh more often? Perhaps it would be a laughable activity simply to gather two or three friends together and brain-storm ways to increase your humor quotient.

Who will you invite?

_____   _____

_____   _____

_____

What steps are you willing to take to activate your endorphins and your sense of feel-good?

_____   _____

_____   _____

_____   _____

CHAPTER 17

Ask Questions and Listen to the Answers

Everyone has a story. One of the most powerful experiences in the world is connecting with another human being at the deep level of shared experiences and feelings. The ability and willingness to reach out to others is a primary avenue to maintain your sense of purpose.

In the world of sales, Harvey Mackay underscores the power of this action. As CEO of Mackay Envelope, this enterprising leader of people employs a team of salespeople who earn more than double the industry's national average. Why? The Mackay 66!

In his book, *Swim with the Sharks Without Being Eaten Alive,* Mackay describes the Mackay Envelope Corporation 66 Question Customer Profile. Every salesperson is trained to build relationships with customers by using the simple techniques of getting to know them personally. The Mackay 66 Questions Profile provides a guide for recording everything from the person's name and address to his or her favorite sports team.[1]

This habit of asking questions and listening to the answers has proved to be very powerful in the world of business.

I think the Timex Corporation must understand this principle as well. Over the last few years the Timex advertising campaign has fascinated me.

Do you remember seeing the full page, color photos of people you have never heard of with a summary about some bizarre event in their lives?

One of my favorites was a picture of a 60-something man with white hair, sparkling blue eyes and rosy cheeks. His story:

"Edwin Robinson became blind and deaf after a truck accident. Nine years later he was struck by lightning and within hours his vision and hearing were restored. Edwin is wearing a . . . Timex!"

At first I wondered why Timex would run an ad like that? But then it dawned on me that everyone has a story, and Timex must really care about normal people, just like you and I, who have stories!

It's true, everyone has a story, which provides a very important clue for experiencing your purpose day by day and for maintaining the wonder and enthusiasm of your Fresh Start.

There is restorative power in the caring and love exchanged when people genuinely tune into one another. Asking questions and listening to the answers produces miraculous serendipities and connections. In fact, I believe

---

1. Harvey Mackay, *Swim with the Sharks Without Being Eaten Alive* (New York: William Morrow and Co., Inc., 1988), 46-53.

that you are where you are at any given time by divine design. It is exciting to look around and see what is unfolding where you are.

The Atlanta Taxi Driver

I recall a cold, wet Tuesday morning in Atlanta. I had completed a program for a client there and needed to get to the airport. When the taxi arrived I stepped into the back of the cab and settled back for the 30 minute ride to Hartsfield International. The driver was a blond man, about 30 years old, who seemed intent on his work.

Abruptly, without really intending to intrude on his work, I surprised myself by asking him, "So, tell me what your long-term goals in life are."

He looked in the rear view mirror to determine the motive behind my question. Satisfied that I had an innocent but vital interest in his future, he responded. "I'd like to compose classical music, but I have a wife and a three-year-old little girl. They are my primary responsibilities right now. However, I haven't given up on my dream."

He paused and then reached across to the passenger seat. Lifting up a large, scholarly book he said, "Whenever I wait for customers, I read and study about classical music."

I was so touched by his dream and his commitment that I shared everything I knew about making dreams reality, including the power of prayer.

When we arrived at the airport, he pulled up in front of the Delta terminal, jumped out, opened the back door and almost lifted me off the back seat of the cab. He gave me a huge bear hug. Two big tears were rolling down his cheeks. "Lady," he said, "you have changed my life."

Now who do you suppose received the greater blessing in that exchange? Every time I share these events my own heart is encouraged and I see his face again in my memory.

These are the serendipities, the renewing encounters, the gifts and surprises awaiting you every day. Life becomes an adventure. Your sense of purpose becomes more evident. You begin to experience the miraculous world of the invisible. Your spirit is renewed.

The La-Z-Boy Furniture Salesman

My mother has been a widow for some time now. In her late 80s, she's still very active in her circle of friends and is considered a bit of a guru among some of her neighbors because she has humorous, encouraging words for her widow friends.

Recently Mom called to say she needed a new La-Z-Boy recliner and wanted me to go with her to help her select the color and style.

As we arrived at the furniture store the salesman greeted us warmly and began giving us a walking tour of the inventory. At one point I stopped him and said, "Tell me your name."

"I'm Harold," he responded.

I introduced myself and my mother, Helen. I then asked, "Where are you from, Harold?"

"Sheldon, Iowa," he said.

I exclaimed that originally Mom was from that part of Iowa. She asked, "Would you happen to know my old boyfriend?"

"I don't know. What was his name?"

My mother recalled the name of her beau of 60 years ago and Harold nearly fainted!

"Why, he's my best friend! I just saw him last month when I was in Sheldon on vacation. You know his wife died about four months ago."

"She did?" There was more than the normal level of

interest in my mother's response to that bit of news!

We bought the recliner. Harold wrote the name, address and phone number of the old boyfriend, and he and Mom began renewing their relationship by mail. Our foray had been more than successful.

After several months of correspondence, Mom's friend asked if he might come to Arizona to visit her for a month or two. It was obvious that he planned to stay at her house.

My mother has a strong sense of traditional standards and she was concerned about what her widow friends would say, so she took an informal community survey. "Bring him in!" they urged her in unison.

This grand gentleman came to visit my mother, and during his stay they renewed friendships with scores of Iowans who also had retired to Arizona. The entire experience brought an expanded sense of joy into my Mom's life.

Ask questions and listen to the answers. Your life-in-the-spirit experiences will be the ongoing benefit of connecting with people.

Dare to reach out to people you don't know. Express genuine interest to know more than their opinion about the stock market or the weather. Listen and learn. Share your own story when it's appropriate. You'll be amazed at the serendipitous experiences that begin to happen.

CHAPTER 18

Practice the Art of Loving

It was a picturesque, *Arizona Highway* kind of sunset. Jim and I were sitting together in the gazebo of our new home in Paradise Valley. Jim was barbecuing his favorite garlic-parmesan chicken. A chilled iceberg salad waited in the refrigerator. It was a perfect evening for romance and intimate conversation. The pink-hued sky was the special effect that produced a sense of wonder. But we weren't watching. We were, instead, having a heated argument over some now-forgotten little stuff. We were both communicating a few decibels above our normal tone, and the intensity was escalating.

Abruptly, divinely, I saw us from another perspective. I transferred out of my soul and into my spirit. The quiet, steady, sincere words that came out of my mouth caught even my attention!

"So what percentage of our marriage do you think is working?"

I had a number in mind, and I was sincerely interested to hear what Jim's evaluation of our situation was.

Jim blinked. He began to shift inwardly also. His answer came in a subdued voice, "Probably 80 to 85 percent is working really well." Those were exactly the percentages I had in mind.

"Why, then, do we keep discussing the issues and concerns in the 15 percent area?"

A tiny smile began to creep across Jim's face. That made me smile. We hugged one another for a while. Then we verbalized the agreement that was our heartfelt resolve. We would consciously begin to talk about and give attention to what was working in our marriage!

This focus on the 80 percent that is working has resulted in a gigantic increase in smiles, tiny steps toward laughter, and a measurable decrease in little-stuff discussions.

Some of the little-stuff discussions at home seem to center around personal preferences. Now we use a shorthand method to halt soul-life, treadmill debates. Let me describe how this might work for you.

You might like a night out at the movies. Your partner may be exhausted and prefer to stay home. They're just small preferences and they can change with circumstances, but on occasion they can be major irritations that escalate into relationship warfare.

> "You never want to do what I want to do! We never get out of the house."
> "That's because you can't sit still for a minute. We always have to be running somewhere, doing something that you've planned."

Sound familiar?

An alternative to mouth-to-mouth combat is simply to ask each other what level of importance their preference is.

"On a scale of 1 to 10, 10 being highest, how important to you is the movie tonight?" The reply might be, "It's a 7. I really had my heart set on seeing this movie and getting out of the house tonight."

The partner might respond, "Staying home tonight for me is only about a 5. I know how much you like to go to the movies. I just get so tired after work, I sometimes don't have the energy to do anything. Let's go out. We could both stand a change of pace.

Notice that both partners have stayed with "I" language and avoided using the accusative "you."

Communicating your emotions by number serves as a practical objectifier and focuses on solutions not on issues. It works when you are in a disagreement over going to the movies or with modes of discipline for your children.

If you want to make a Fresh Start in your relationship, this can serve as a powerful tool for keeping your commitment and for living out of your spirit rather than living out of the trap of the soul emotions.

Loving Leadership in the Corporate Environment

Max DePree, CEO at Herman Miller, Inc., talks about the need for sensitive caring in corporate America. In his book, *Leadership Is an Art,* he describes an incident in which he became choked up while reading a touching letter from the mother of one of his handicapped employees. He writes:

"I almost got through this letter, but could not finish. There I stood in front of this group of people— some of them pretty hard-driving—tongue-tied and embarrassed, unable to continue. At that point one of our senior vice-presidents, Joe Schwartz—

urbane, elegant, mature—strode up the center aisle, put his arm around my shoulder, kissed me on the cheek, and adjourned the meeting."[1]

DePree states, "Intimacy is at the heart of competence . . . Above all, intimacy rises from, and gives rise to, strong relationships. Intimacy is one way of describing the relationship we all desire with work."[2]

People everywhere long to be loved and recognized. Considering the amount of hours devoted to work in one's lifetime it is obvious that the workplace needs to be a place where leadership springs from the spirit. This critical action involves being willing to be personally vulnerable and daring to transfer out of the mind games so evident in corporate politics.

What actions could you take to move toward demonstrating your care for others in your work environment?

_____

_____

_____

Practical Expressions of Love

There are infinite ways to express our love and appreciation for others. Many times we fail to act on our feelings because of the frenetic activity cycle or because of fear of feeling foolish, or appearing weak or being rejected, etc.

Nevertheless, expressing genuine feelings of love and appreciation is one of the most personally restoring activities you can practice.

---

1. Max DePree, *Leadership Is an Art* (New York: Doubleday, 1989), 124.
2. DePree, 45, 49.

Practice your creativity by making a list of 15 unique activities to express your feelings for someone in your family, for an employee, a colleague or the teller at the bank.

_____	_____	_____
_____	_____	_____
_____	_____	_____
_____	_____	_____
_____	_____	_____

An additional exercise to reinforce this critical action in your life would be to brainstorm 15 to 20 more ideas with a good friend or a loved one.

My youngest daughter, Michelle, lives in California so we often exchange our expression of love via long-distance, late-night phone calls and short, encouraging notes to one another. We share our successes, failures and concerns.

After one of our conversations in which I had described an upcoming challenging presentation, Michelle sent me a Shoebox greeting card.

I was going to hire a skywriter to write high overhead all the reasons why I love you, but I ran into a teensy, weensy, little problem . . . The sky's not big enough.

She added:

Mom, I just wanted to bring you a little sunshine in what might be a busy, stressful day.

I love you so much! I think of you every moment. We are so lucky to know we are just passing through this place, on to something beautiful and timeless. It makes me happy to know we will be together forever. I guess that's what makes everyday bearable! I pray that God will fill you with peace, joy and happiness.

I'm looking forward to being together soon—flesh and blood!

My heart bursts over you!

O X,
Michelle

My spirit soars whenever I reread Michelle's words. These gifts of love renew both the giver and the receiver.

Who are some of the people who need to be recipients of your practical expressions of love?

_____   _____   _____

_____   _____   _____

_____   _____   _____

CHAPTER 19

Define Your Purpose in Life

Corporate America has spent millions and millions of dollars and thousands of hours of labor and brainpower creating mission statements. Virtually every major organization and many entrepreneurial companies have become clear, at least on paper, about their purpose for being in business.

Often the mission or vision statements are framed and hung on the wall, as well as printed in annual reports and marketing brochures.

Some of the standard phrases are:

- "committed to the well-being and empowerment of our employees"
- "committed to providing extraordinary service based on quality and excellence in our products and our people"
- "demonstrating respect for the individual and integrity in the marketplace"

- "with a vision for becoming the global leader in the production of . . ."

As a business consultant, it has always seemed to me that this focus on the corporate mission or purpose is only addressing surface (soul-life) issues. The spirit of a company springs from individual lives within the company, and few leaders seem to be starting from the spirit of the individual. Imagine a corporation filled with individuals who know what their personal purpose in life is!

Kevin McCarthy, my friend and colleague, has written a powerful, challenging book, The *On-Purpose Person*. The main character in Kevin's book is on a search for purpose in his life. He meets a wise man who gives him this advice:

"Remember, our purpose is within us and permanent. It will take time to unearth it . . . Be expectant and exploring. As you move boldly in the direction of your wants, your purpose will emerge in time. Keep looking for it and you'll find it." [1]

Kevin challenges the reader, through a series of fascinating exercises, to think clearly about personal purpose. He suggests a distinguishing difference between purpose and vision, mission and values. You may find, as I did, these questions from his book to be very helpful as you begin to create your own statement of purpose in life. [2]

- Why do I exist? (Purpose Statement)
- How am I to live out my purpose in regard to specific areas of my life today? (Mission Statement)

Notice that the first question addresses internal issues (spirit) and the second one addresses external actions (transformed soul-life and body-life).

---

1. Kevin McCarthy, *The On-Purpose Person* (Colorado Springs: Piñon Press, NavPress Publishing Group, 1992), 91.
2. McCarthy, 82-86.

His questions provide a valuable starting point for you to begin to formulate your own answers. Some of your responses in earlier chapters have prepared you for this endeavor. Remember your purpose is hidden in the center of your wants, desires, interests and values.

The Life of Terri Barley

Sometimes we get stuck in the idea that we can't be an on-purpose person unless we're someone like Mother Teresa! Not true! That's the chaotic mind at work, trying to make you feel purposeless, like a speck on the face of the planet. After all, it reasons, you haven't been on the cover of *Time* magazine, and you didn't discover the polio vaccine.

That's an outside-in way of measuring success!

Let me share a different perspective with you. After giving a management seminar for a large restaurant chain, I joined the attendees for the evening banquet. I selected a seat near the back of the room, at a table set for eight. A few minutes later, one of the regional managers sat down next to me. He looked slightly surprised to see me.

"I'm amazed! I actually prayed I'd get to talk to you today. But there never seemed to be an opportunity," he said, and introduced himself as Jim Barley. I was aware of his physical fitness, his good looks and his aura of success. He appeared to be in his mid-30s. His people skills were obvious, and I knew he was a key person in the company. We exchanged initial pleasantries, and then Jim asked if he could share a very personal story.

Jim began by showing me a picture of his beautiful wife Terri and his two young children. He explained what a great family life they shared. He and Terri were avid tennis players and spent many relaxing, laughter-filled moments on the courts together.

Eight weeks earlier Terri had gone to Nevada to visit her parents. While there she suddenly and unexpectedly was stricken with a brain aneurysm and died. As Jim recounted the story he was visibly shaken by this tragedy in what had been an ideal life. He said that the priest at their church had called and suggested that he, Jim, speak at the memorial service for Terri. Jim described his reticence to consider doing that. He was understandably concerned about his own ability to communicate without breaking up emotionally.

"No one knew Terri better than I did. I felt I wanted to share with others what a special person she was. So, I began to prepare my remarks. I began to look through some of Terri's personal things and stumbled upon her Bible. Resting in the pages of the Book was a small note in Terri's handwriting. It seems important to me to share her words with you, Glenna."

Jim reached inside his suit pocket and brought out a program from Terri's Memorial mass. In it was printed Terri's note.

Dear God,

I feel you have called me for many things. First of all to be a kind, gentle and loving mother and wife. To be a confidante for friends who may need me to listen and advise. A strength for the family members who are still searching for you and are not sure of when or what they have been called for. Also, to be a strength of character for those with whom I may have contact, in even a most casual way, to let them know that Christ is still alive in me and in this world.

Terri Barley

As I finished reading Terri's clearly defined purpose in life, Jim Barley made this observation.

"Terri's death was God's powerful touch on my life. For the first time I saw clearly what Terri had tried to communicate to me all the years of our marriage. She fulfilled her purpose in a way she would never have imagined. Perhaps you can share Terri's story as you speak and others can continue to be touched by Terri's life, even in her death."

As you read Terri's story I cannot help but think you will be moved along in your own pursuit of becoming very clear about your calling in life. It is encouraging to realize again that each of us has been created for a purpose. It is not about fame or fortune or field of endeavor. It is simply about discovering our own personal reason for being.

Terri's purpose statement might well have been, "to let people know that Christ is alive in me and in this world."

Her mission statement might well have been, "to be a kind, gentle and loving mother and wife. To be a confidante for friends . . . a strength for family members." These are the external, visible demonstrations of her internal sense of calling or purpose.

Your Purpose

Your authentic purpose in life is often intricately related to your passion or passions. My father's passionate love for people fueled his sense of purpose. He had a deep desire to make people glad they saw him. This desire was planted in his heart by the Creator. The practical expression of that desire was absolutely congruent with who he was. He was living from the inside-out.

Your passions and values are often closely related but not always identical. For example, I consider knowledge to be a personal passion of mine. It is also one of my key values. On the other hand, I value time but I am not passionate about time. (Someone who teaches time management may value time and be passionate about time as well!)

Perhaps a distinguishing element is the fact that you are more actively involved in your passion and emotionally committed to your values. Both impact your purpose.

Mother Teresa would be a classic example of a person whose purpose in life is directly tied to her passion. She is actively fulfilling her purpose by outwardly providing care and dignity for the dying. She has a passionate heart for people and this is intricately related to the value she places on human life.

If you have followed the life of this amazing woman you have seen the power that flows out of an on-purpose life. Here is a woman who in her 80s, living in severe circumstances much of the time, demonstrates:

- High energy
- Laser-beam focus
- Inner peace; a sense of knowing
- Personal joy; inner satisfaction
- An abundant supply of love
- An incredible charisma
- A life-changing impact on individual people and the world

These are the qualities you will begin to experience as you become clear about your own purpose in life.

Begin now to put words to your sense of inner being:

It seems to me that my purpose in life is related to

_____

_____

_____

The way I feel compelled to live this out in my life is by

_____

_____

_____

_____

As you become clearer about your purpose and your mission, these will be the calibrating factors for all of your choices. All of your decisions will become simplified because they are regulated by your purpose. You will begin to experience increasingly the attributes apparent in an on-purpose life.

To keep your purpose clearly before you, consider carrying your purpose statement in your wallet and framing it to hang on your wall. When the outside pressures come, you can remember who you are and why you are.

The Heart of the Fresh Start!

For more than 15 years I have been speaking to companies and associations nationally and internationally. I have provided practical suggestions for improved customer service, fresh insights into leadership development and some thought-provoking keynotes designed to awaken the hearts of listeners.

But it isn't enough. The key ingredient is always missing from my printed outlines and handouts. And that is understandable. The paid professional presenter needs to honor the diversity of belief systems within an audience.

However, the Spirit of God still finds ways to speak to hearts. The result is that many employees and conference attendees want to discuss life in the Spirit at a deeper level. Their questions reflect their thirst for the inside-out life experience. They long for authentic life. Many have seen corporate mission statements on the walls of the halls that are not lived out in the lives of the leaders. They have listened to speeches on the corporate "Vision" and watched leaders who can't see the need to recognize the efforts of his or her own team members. Quite simply, the walk and talk are not a match. This is outside-in leadership.

In his book *Leadership Jazz*, Max DePree, CEO of Herman Miller, Inc., recounts the true story of his granddaughter Zoe and, in so doing, illustrates the life of an inside-out leader.

Max explains that Zoe was born prematurely, weighing 1 pound, 7 ounces. She was given a 10 percent chance of living three to five days. Zoe's birth father had abandoned the family, so Ruth, the nurse, enlisted Max to function as a surrogate father. She asked that he come to see Zoe every day, to rub her legs, arms and body ever so gently with the tip of his finger. As he touched her he was to express aloud his love for her, daily.

"Ruth was doing exactly the right thing on Zoe's behalf," DePree writes, "and, of course, on my behalf as well. Without realizing it she was giving me one of the best possible descriptions of the work of a leader. At the core of becoming a leader is the need always to connect one's voice and one's touch."[3]

As the CEO of one of America's finest companies, Max DePree is an example of the inside-out life. This doesn't mean he makes only wise decisions or is always perfect with his people. Rather, it means that he has a sense about the Spirit that empowers his soul and body to be more than a carcass going through the motions. People feel the difference.

---

3. Max DePree, *Leadership Jazz* (New York: Doubleday, 1992), 2, 3.

The authenticity of this kind of leadership inspires productivity and integrity. It instills enthusiasm and team spirit. The results include improved customer service, caring, astute leadership and the enhanced morale which perpetuates the productivity, the service and the enthusiasm.

But we have removed this key ingredient from the workplace and the result has been greed, griping and grasping for a sense of purpose. The prophet wrote "Where there is no vision the people perish." (The Hebrew original actually can be read as, "Where there is no vision the people go wild!")[4]

Remembering Your Purpose in the Midst of Change

Currently the work environment in America has a high percentage of fear, disillusionment, low morale and a lackluster attitude about work itself. The ongoing changes related to downsizing, rightsizing and reengineering have resulted in a large display of insecurity, cynicism, lack of loyalty and very little pride in one's work.

Individuals have, in the past, been able to count on company stability, promotions based on good performance and a consistent work environment. The crumbling of this foundation is a wake-up call. Employees who once counted on a secure financial future or a sense of purpose in a career have awakened to find themselves standing on shifting sand.

One out of every three workers in the United States is a temporary worker. Predictions indicate two out of three workers will be temporaries by the year 2000. The largest private employer in the United States is Manpower, Inc., with nearly 600.000 employees.[5]

---

4. Prov. 29:18.
5. Lance Morrow, "The Temping of America," *Time*, 29 March 1993: 41-47.

You may be one of those who has come to realize that you were so busy building a career you failed to build a life. You may even feel betrayed or at least confused as a result of this upheaval. If you are seeing the folly of counting on a company, a career or a coveted position in the corporate structure, you are ready for a Fresh Start!

Families have suffered because of the preoccupation with the outside-in life. Perhaps you are a parent who needs to make some adjustments. No doubt a changing world continues to impact you both personally and professionally. The steadying factor is clarity of purpose and vision. This is the heart of your Fresh Start!

Summary of Book Two

You have now discovered nine ways to maintain and sustain your Fresh Start. What practical steps are you taking, even as you close the pages of this book, to enhance your life experience?

The Art of the Fresh Start has been designed to nudge you forward in your deepest longings for a meaningful life. May that be your experience.

Epilogue

You may recall that I mentioned in Chapter One that I learned about miracles at the age of 21, and learned about hope from my father over a lifetime.

One of the major lessons I learned out of what happened in my life was this:

We all have turning points in our journey through life. Almost always, the clues to who we are and why we are here are hidden in those turning points. They can be tragic, triumphant, bizarre or simply significant in the moment, but they contain God's messages to us. God engineers the DNA, the desires and the details to lead us into our purpose.

When I was a senior at Northwestern University my parents, in their early 50s at the time, experienced their first real understanding of the Person of Christ. They became enthusiastic Christians.

I, on the other hand, had become an enthusiastic, existential agnostic at the university. This divergence of opinion and understanding led to major philosophical problems when I went home for Thanksgiving vacation in 1958. My father, true to his wisdom and grace, challenged my intellectual fervor. "Why don't you return to the university and discover all the proofs that the Bible is not the Word of God and that Jesus is not God. We can discuss your findings at Christmas."

The next few weeks of research produced my own turning point in life. As I visited with one of the scientists at the Technological Institute at Northwestern, I discovered the mountains of scientific, geological and archaeological information which support the validity of the Old and New Testament.

When I opened the Gospel of John I saw clearly, in the very first words of the book, that Jesus is God and Creator of all things according to the written record.

I was faced with a dilemma. Integrity of thought required that I must either believe all or none of the contents of the Book. To pick and choose what made sense to me was to elevate myself to the position of being the All-Knowing One.

The resolution for me was to challenge the One who claimed to be the Truth. Quietly I asked Jesus Christ to make Himself known to me as God if indeed He was. The sky did not collapse nor was I struck by lightning, but for me there came a deep knowing that the Lord of Creation had become a human being in history and His Spirit had taken up residence in my spirit during my 21st year of life.

This was the turning point that has held the key to my calling. God's wisdom, energy, love and grace compel me to bring Life to others. It is my sincere prayer that your faith and life have been enriched by the words I have shared.

May the Fresh Start that revolutionized my life hold great significance for your own Fresh Start.

Warmly,

Glenna

Author's Note

If you have been touched by the contents of this book, please feel free to write to me personally and share the results in your life. Or, you may have comments and suggestions for me to incorporate into my next books. I will treasure your response.

I will be happy to put you on my mailing list for a complimentary newsletter and announcements about my upcoming books and seminars.

If you would like information about my turning point of faith please mention that. I will be happy to send you the expanded version of that experience!

For any of this information, or for information on how to have me provide a keynote address or seminar at your next event, contact:

Glenna Salsbury
P.O. Box 12009
Scottsdale, Arizona 85267
Call 602-483-7732
FAX: 602-483-2615

Appendix One

Body, Soul, Spirit

When I speak of body, soul and spirit, I am describing the tripartite nature of humanity based on biblical usage. In I Thessalonians 5:23 the Apostle Paul distinguishes the three when he says, "I pray God your whole spirit and soul and body be preserved blameless unto the coming of our Lord Jesus Christ." Here he uses the Greek form *pneuma* for spirit, *psuche* for soul, and *soma* for body.

There are two significant parts in this passage. First there is a distinction among the three elements of humans. However, there is also a definite reference to the wholeness, the unity, the importance of the oneness of the three.

In Hebrews 4:12 the author writes, "the word of God is quick and powerful, and sharper than any two-edged sword piercing even to the dividing asunder of soul and spirit and of the joints and the marrow, and is a discerner of the thoughts and intents of the heart."

Once again there is a clear distinction among the three. Yet the inherent wholeness is so complete that only the Word of God can, by revelation, divide or separate one from another.

In I Corinthians 2:13-15 Paul uses terms that are very helpful for clarifying the Greek usage of these terms. "But the natural man [*psuchikos*] receiveth not the things of the Spirit of God, for they are foolishness to him, neither can he know them, because they are spiritually [*pneumatikos*] discerned."

This passage recognizes the soul life that is not filled with the *pneumatikos*, the life of the spirit, has no discernment. The source for wisdom is in the spirit.

Psuche is the only word translated soul in the New Testament. *Pneuma* occurs 379 times and is translated spirit each time. In the Old Testament, Genesis 2:7 reads, "God breathed into Adam the breath of life (*pneuma* is ruach in Hebrew) and he became a living soul (*psuche* is *nephesh* in Hebrew)." In other words, man had a body and a soul that received life from the Spirit.

In summary, a whole, congruent person is one who is fully integrated in body, soul and spirit. This life in the spirit transforms the body and soul to produce this wholeness. It is a God-breathed life.

Note: See Appendix Two for a discussion of mind.

Appendix Two

Mind

The traditional Hebrew and Greek perspectives on the mind, as outlined in the Old and New Testament, clearly support the chaotic state of an unrenewed mind. The Spirit of God acting upon the mind of man transforms the chaos.

Psalm 94:11 "The Lord knoweth the thoughts of man that they are vanity."

Proverbs 23:7 "As a man thinketh in his heart so is he."

The word "heart" is the Hebrew word *nephesh* that is also regularly translated "soul." Thus, the "soul" and the "heart" of man are depicted as the source for thoughts.

Matthew 15:18a "For out of the heart proceed evil thoughts."

Romans 8:6-7a "For to be carnally minded is death, but to be spiritually minded is life and peace. Because the carnal mind is enmity against God . . ."

The mind, in its natural state, *psuche*, is chaotic, filled with fear, rebellion, reactions, negative desires. The spiritually renewed mind, *pneumatik*, has been transformed by the Spirit of God at work on man's spirit which affects the soul . . . the source of thought-life.

Romans 12:2a "And be not conformed to this world but be ye transformed by the renewing of your mind . . ."

There definitely is a clear indication that the soul-life in its natural state needs help. The help is accomplished through the order and simplicity supplied by the Spirit.

Isaiah 55:8-9 "For my thoughts are not your thoughts, neither are your ways my ways saith the Lord. For as the heavens are higher than the earth, so are my ways higher than your ways and my thoughts higher than your thoughts."

Isaiah 26:3 "Thou wilt keep him in perfect peace whose mind is stayed on thee."

Bibliography

Berkeley Version, The Bible. Grand Rapids: Zondervan Publishing, 1962.

Canfield, Jack and Mark Victor Hansen. *Chicken Soup for the Soul*. Deerfield Beach: Health Communications, Inc., 1993

Carnegie, Dale. *How to Stop Worrying and Start Living* New York: Pocket Books, 1985.

Crum, Thomas F. *The Magic of Conflict*. New York: Simon and Schuster, 1988.

DePree, Max. *Leadership Is an Art*. New York: Doubleday, 1989.

——. *Leadership Jazz*. New York: Doubleday, 1992.

Emery, Gary and Pat Emery. *Second Force*. New York: NAL-Dutton, 1990.

Hunter, Thom. *Those Not-So-Still Small Voices*. Colorado Springs: NavPress, 1993.

Keller, Werner. *The Bible As History.* New York: William Morrow & Co., 1964.

King James Version, *The Bible.* Nashville: Thomas Nelson Publishing, 1976.

Mackay, Harvey. *Swim with the Sharks Without Being Eaten Alive.* New York: William Morrow and Co., Inc., 1988.

McCarthy, Kevin. *The On-Purpose Person.* Colorado Springs: Piñon Press, NavPress Publishing Group, 1992.

Naisbett, John and Patricia Aburdene. *Megatrends 2000.* New York: William Morrow and Co., 1990.

Prather, Hugh. *Notes to Myself.* New York: Bantam, 1990.

Rhode, Naomi. *More Beautiful Than Diamonds.* Nashville: Thomas Nelson Publishers, 1991.

Rosanoff, Nancy. *The Intuition Workout.* New York: Aslan Publishing, 1991.

Senge, Peter. *The Fifth Discipline.* New York: Doubleday/Currency, 1990.

Stoddard, Alexandra. *Living the Beautiful Life.* New York: Avon Books, 1986.

Stratford, Sherman. "Leaders Learn to Heed the Voice Within." *Fortune*: August 22, 1994: 92-93.

Tipler, Frank. *The Physics of Immortality.* New York: Doubleday, 1994.

HCI's Business Self-Help Books Motivate and Inspire

The Master Motivator
Secrets of Inspiring Leadership
Mark Victor Hansen and Joe Batten

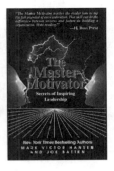

Here is the definitive book on motivating others from two of the world's most renowned and respected motivational speakers. Joe Batten—mentor to Ross Perot and author of *Tough-Minded Management*—and Mark Victor Hansen—motivator/communicator extraordinaire and co-author of the best-selling *Chicken Soup for the Soul* series—show you how to achieve top performance from yourself and those you lead.
Code 3553 . . . . $9.95

How to Turn Business & Financial Relationships into Fun & Profit
Anne Boe
Author of *Is Your Net-Working?*

Networking Success
How to Turn Business & Financial Relationships into Fun & Profit
Anne Boe

Networking is the business tool of 1990s that separates the successful from the unsuccessful. Along with networking's unquestioned value in business, it's also useful in personal relationships. Here master networker Anne Boe describes ideas for developing, nurturing and growing your relationships, financial contacts and career networks for peak performance on and off the job.
Code 3650 . . . . $12.95

What You Want, Wants You
How to Get Out of Your Rut
Debra Jones

People in the 1990s are reevaluating their lifestyles as never before. Many workers are rethinking their career choices to be more in tune with what they really want to do. Here Debra Jones, marketing whiz extraordinaire, gives you a game plan for digging yourself out of the quagmire of indecision and hopelessness in order to find your life path. An inspiring book that will leave you revitalized.
Code 3677 . . . . $9.95

The Art of the Fresh Start
How to Make and Keep Your New Year's Resolutions for a Lifetime
Glenna Salsbury

In the #1 *New York Times* bestseller *Chicken Soup for the Soul*, Glenna Salsbury told the story of her dreams becoming reality. Now she shares her practical, step-by-step approach for tapping into your core being to achieve permanent, repeatable and ongoing self-renewal. This unique approach to goal-setting through internal and spiritual guidance will teach you to live a life filled with hope, joy and a multitude of fresh starts.
Code 3642 . . . . $9.95

Available at your favorite bookstore or call 1-800-441-5569 for Visa or MasterCard orders.
Prices do not include shipping and handling. Your response code is HCI.

Share the Magic of Chicken Soup

Lift Your Spirits with
Chicken Soup for the Soul Audiotapes

World-renowned inspirational speakers Jack Canfield and Mark Victor Hansen share stories from their two *New York Times* bestsellers *Chicken Soup for the Soul* and *A 2nd Helping of Chicken Soup for the Soul* on these heartwarming audiotapes.

The Best of the Original Chicken Soup for the Soul Audiotape

This single 90-minute cassette contains the very best stories from the ABBY award-winning *Chicken Soup for the Soul*. You will be enlightened and entertained by the masterful storytelling of Jack and Mark and friends. The essential stories are all here.

Code 3723: One 90-minute audiocassette $9.95

Chicken Soup for the Soul Audio Gift Set

This six-tape set includes the entire audio collection of stories from *Chicken Soup for the Soul*, over seven hours of listening pleasure. The inspirational message spoken in this set will not only enhance your commute to and from work, it will also leave you in a positive frame of mind the whole day. Listen to these tapes at home and be uplifted by the insights and wisdom of these emotionally powerful stories. A wonderful gift for friends, loved ones or yourself.

Code 3103: Six cassettes—7 hours of inspiration . . $29.95

A 2nd Helping of Chicken Soup for the Soul Abridged Version Audiotape

The newest collection of *Chicken Soup* stories, straight from the sequel. This two-tape volume brings to you the authors' favorite stories from *A 2nd Helping of Chicken Soup for the Soul*. Now you can listen to the newest batch in your car or in the comfort of your own home. Fresh stories to brighten your day!

Code 3766: Two 90-minute cassettes $14.95

Available at your favorite bookstore or call 1-800-441-5569 for Visa or MasterCard orders. Prices do not include shipping and handling. Your response code is HCI.

STORY BOOKS TO ENLIGHTEN AND ENTERTAIN

Catch the Whisper of the Wind
Collected Stories and Proverbs from Native Americans
Cheewa James

The richness of Native American culture is explored by noted motivational speaker and broadcast journalist Cheewa James. These provocative stories touch the heart and offer deep insight into the soul of the Indian.
Code 3693 . . . .$9.95

The 7th Floor Ain't Too High for Angels to Fly
A Collection of Stories on Relationships and Self-Understanding
John M. Eades, Ph.D.

In this diverse collection of provocative stories, therapist John Eades helps readers to reflect on how they are living their own lives and invites them to discover the inner resources that lead to true joy and fulfillment. You'll laugh and cry, but you won't be able to put down *The 7th Floor Ain't Too High for Angels to Fly.*
Code 3561 . . . .$10.95

Bedtime Stories for Grown-ups
Fairy-Tale Psychology
Sue Gallehugh, Ph.D. and Allen Gallehugh

In this witty, fully illustrated book, therapist Sue Gallehugh and her son Allen adapt classic fairy tales to illustrate the fundamental principles of self-love through mental health and psychological growth. This upbeat, entertaining book will leave readers laughing out loud as they explore the value of the serious concept of self-worth.
Code 3618 . . . .$9.95

Values from the Heartland
Stories of an American Farmgirl
Bettie B. Youngs, Ph.D., Ed.D

One of the best-loved authors from *Chicken Soup for the Soul* shares uplifting, heartwarming tales, culled from her memories of growing up on a farm in Iowa. These value-laden stories will show you how hard times, when leavened with love and support, can provide strength of character, courage and leadership.
Code 3359: paperback $11.95
Code 3340: hard cover $22.00

Mentors, Masters and Mrs. MacGregor
Stories of Teachers Making a Difference
Jane Bluestein, Ph.D.

Jane Bluestein asked celebrities and common folks around the world the following question: Who is that one special teacher that made a difference in your life? The collected answers to this question make up this truly touching book which will appeal to the student—and the teacher—in all of us.
Code 3375: paperback $11.95
Code 3367: hard cover $22.00

Available at your favorite bookstore or call 1-800-441-5569 for Visa or MasterCard orders.
Prices do not include shipping and handling. Your response code is HCI.